Self-Hypnosis and Post-Hypnotic Suggestions

by
DR. GLENN VAN WARREBEY

Professor of Psychology at Delaware Valley Community College, Matamoras, Pa.; Therapist and Hypnotherapist at the Holistic Health Clinic in Ogdensburg, N.J.; Member of the New Jersey Branch of The American Society of Clinical Hypnosis.

Published by
THEO. GAUS, LTD.
30 Prince St., Brooklyn, N.Y. 11201

ISBN 089260-118-3 (HB)
LC# 77-94104

TABLE OF CONTENTS

Overview - Part 1

Method - Part 2

This Poem is Dedicated to the Young Snowflake:

SPRING TO MORE SPRING

In our flight through the cosmos and clouds,
we see a beautiful and intricate snowflake
floating into the origin and eternal stream.
Though the stream is our eventual destination,
we do not have to make the liquid transition
quite so early...
Upon reaching the earth, we rest upon mountain's leaf,
inertly waiting for our spring to come.
Moving, we wait for the symphonious sun and
pure homeostasis of our minds merging with
the warmth of Total Unity...
It is, thus, a most positive transcendence
for the young snowflake...
A direct unifying experience with the flow of life
and God's All One.
A wing flutters, the stream empties into the sea
and the sea, the sky...
The moldless mold spontaneously bursts open and
a new snowflake is reborn.
This time, it is even more radiant in symmetry,
as it falls freely toward its leaf...

- G. V. W.

THIS BOOK IS DEDICATED
to My Understanding and Supportive
Parents
GLENN and ELEANOR
and to JANET
I Give My Sincere Wish for
Mutual Development, Understanding,
and Patience

AUTHOR'S PREFACE

Jigero Kano makes an excellent statement about Judo (literally translated, the "Gentle Way"), an art which he founded. He maintains that the principle of "maximum-efficient-use" of the mind and body is basic to all techniques in Judo. This same principle can be applied to the mind-body in the science of hypnotism, synthesizing an education of the physical, mental and moral elements of the individual.

The profound spiritual and philosophical dimension of Zen acts as a catalyst to the Way ("do" or "Tao") of hypnosis. As a paradigm defines the art or science in which it operates, it is conceivable that Zen could be seen as a paradigm for the psycho-spiritual element of hypnosis, and hypnosis could be seen as a paradigm of psychotherapeutic Zen...a kind of "goal achieving" Za Zen meditation. Judo could be seen as the result of hypnosis and Zen expressed in movement and action.

If one defines education as a growth and learning experience and adds a therapeutic emphasis to it, a form of psychotherapy is then manifested. The principles of Zen, hypnotism and Judo have a significant therapeutic and educative potential. This potential is holistic, as it views and integrates the psychosoma as One.

The perspective of Zen and hypnosis (as well as of Judo) marks a Way of Life that is therapeutic, holistic and existentially valid. The notion of gentleness and of flowing with the currents of life are psychologically and viscerally present, not theorized or intellectualized. The "Watercourse Way" is a Way of Taoism which is also central to all three. In hypnotism, Zen and the "Gentle Way" the weak paradoxically overcome the strong. Thus, in the spring, water wears down the stone.

The Judoka (Judo student) or hypnosis subject learns to flow with the Tao of the science in which he is involved. When he is successful and incorporates this into his Way (Tao) of life, he becomes much more adaptive. When one increases his adaptability, lives an existentially valid Way (Tao) of life and improves himself psychologically, he is at the same time in a process of inner directed psychotherapy. In this case, self-hypnosis may be called a psychotherapy of self by self, and Judo a psychotherapy in motion.

In addition to the complementarity of Eastern philosophy, Judo, and hypnotism, there is a central element of self-improvement which is explicit in this book. The self-mastery that is derived from self-hypnosis is a noteworthy benefit and indeed a delight. Everyone in the world has an aspect (or aspects) of himself which needs improvement. This human quality is "simply profound." It is simple because it is a commonality of the species...we are not perfect machines! It is profound because self-mastery ultimately leads to the refinement of an aware, polished and integrated individual. Self-knowledge is another salient factor. When a person truly becomes aware, understanding his reasoning, motives and drives on both a subconscious and conscious level, he has taken a foundational and mammoth step toward self-improvement. Hence, in so many cases, self-knowledge begets self-improvement and self-mastery. In time, the colossal potential power of the mind becomes realized, self-fulfilled and actualized in a beneficial and therapeutic way.

It is my intention to explore these notions in the following pages. I sincerely hope that you enjoy this exploration and that you may benefit and improve yourself by fusing the principles of Zen, Judo and hypnotism into your Tao of Life.

Glenn Van Warrebey, Psy. D.

ACKNOWLEDGMENTS

A special acknowledgement is made to The Institute for Psycho-Integrity in Flanders, New Jersey and to The Family Counseling Center in Bradenton, Florida. Also, I would like to fully acknowledge the authors cited herein. I further wish to sincerely thank both Lynn Kraft for her immeasureable help with the typing and Maureen Babula for her careful editing and "warm friendship."

The following are fine individuals, whom I sincerely appreciate knowing and wholeheartedly acknowledge. For they through time and space relative to my being, have been a nexus of inspiration. Amidst the profanity and thorns of life, they flower, and by doing so shed the essence of light and right to others, as they transcend the shadows. They are the egregious white eagles who fly high in the clouds. They warm the external gelidity of existence. Unlike the common man who puts others down to falsely think himself up, these put others up and gracefully reach down. Because of men like these, who are respected without rank status, society grows and flourishes....Namaste!

A. C. Aldana, M.D.
Jerome Amend, Ph.D.
Harry Arons
Robert Austin
Claus Bahnson, M.D.
Percy Balentine, B.A.

B. Bewley, M.A.
E. Borden
A. M. Brunzlick
Albert Buschmann, LLB.
L. Buschmann, B.A.
J. L. Byrne

Charles Cassidy, M.Div.
Tom Connlly, M.A.
L. Jerry Cunningham, Ph.D.
Anu DeMonterice, M.D.
Robert DeVoe, M.A.
Bernard Feeney, Rev.
Raymond Feinberg, D.D.S.
Erich Fromm, Ph.D.
Robert Garth, D.C.
James Geffken
C. G. Gilsdorf
Jan Grinsland
R. G. Greene
Don Hammel
Robert Hansen, B.A.
George Harris, M.A.
Russ M. Harrison
Robert Harte
James Hedstrom, Ph.D.
R. T. Higgins
Joe Hoffman, J.D.
Robert Holland, Ed.D.
Steve Houghten, B.A.
Inn Soo Hwong, M.A.
Richard Jacoby, Ph.D.
William Janish
Henry Johnson, Ph.D.
Al Kaders, M.A.
Lance Kirtland
H. Koblenzer, M.D.
Philip Kurtz, D.M.D.
Lawrence Lentchner, Ph.D.
William Liggett, M.A.
Jan Lindhorst, Th.D.
John Lombardi, D.D.S.
Sherman Masten, Ph.D.
James Mills, Ph.D.
Greg Molar, M.A.
D. Moltini
Dan Montgomery, Ph.D.
John Murray, M.A.

T. J. Norris, D.C.
Rodney Odell, M.A.
H. F. O'Gorman, D.D.S.
Frank Pack, Ph.D.
Charles Pierce, M.A.
Thomas Pivnichny, M.A.
Phil Porter, M.A.
Melvin Powers
Robert Powers, M.D.
Roger Raskopf, Ph.D.
L. A. Rauls
John Reiniger, M.A.
L. Robbins, Ph.D.
Pat Robertson, Rev.
Richard C. Roby, Ph.D.
Dieter Rosellen
Jay Sanford, M.A.
B. B. Scarborough, Ph.D.
William Schumacher
K. H. Schwartzman
George H. Smith, Ph.D.
Reg Sheldrick, Ph.D.
George H. Smith, Ph.D.
Richard Sorensen
Lawrence Spiegel, Ph.D.
J. N. Sterrit
Patrick Touhy
A. Van Beek
Pierrot Van Tiggelen, Ph.D.
Rene Van Tiggelen, M.D.
Wayne Van Warrebey, R.H.
Ben Velthoven, B.A.
Fritz Ward, M.A.
N. E. Wardle
Herbert Weininger, M.D.
Robert Weinstein, M.D.
S. A. West, B.A.
Robert White, Ph.D.
Robert Widmar, M.A.
W. E. Wielechowski, D.C.
Y. Yonezuka, M.A.

A FOREWORD FROM A PSYCHIATRIST

For such a long time, there has been an unfulfilled need in the applied as well as the academic world for a book like this. Dr. Van Warrebey has well integrated theory with application and hypothesis with life experience. The book is richly informative and rather extraordinary! It has a multi-dimensional, fresh and insightful perspective which distinguishes it above many others on the subject.

I believe many general practitioners would agree that 80-90% of their patients' physical symptoms are directly attributable to psychological and emotional factors. In many cases, medication is not the answer.

Frequently symptoms and other pathology diagnosed as acne, psoriasis, arthritis, impotency, insomnia, high blood pressure, menstrual cramps, allergies, ulcers, asthma and much more are clearly psychosomatic. Often, these seemingly "organic" problems can be resolved by the use of hypnosis without the sometimes negative effects of medication and drug dependency.

Sometimes post-hypnotic suggestions can reproduce the positive effects of a medication without its often undesirable side effects. An important point Dr. Van Warrebey brings out is that self-hypnosis can help the whole person psychologically, physically and even spiritually. The notion of self-mastery through self-hypnosis is a viable alternative to the unnecessary use of medication and an adjunct to psychiatry and psychotherapy. I am extremely enthusiastic about this book and would recommend it and the record album to patients, psychiatrists, psychologists, social workers and others in the helping professions.

Habiba A. Koblenzer, M.D.,
Psychiatrist in Private Practice,
President of the New Jersey
Society of Clinical Hypnosis,
a component section of the
American Society of Clinical
Hypnosis.

A FOREWORD FROM A PSYCHOLOGIST AND MARRIAGE COUNSELOR

There is a good deal of emerging interest in the field of hypnosis. It is almost a renaissance, springing from the realization that hypnosis is indeed a real and a legitimately powerful part of a professional therapist's psychotherapeutic armamentarium. Freud's disenchantment with hypnosis because it was not a universal panacea, coupled with the advent of fictional novels, such as Svengali's portrayal of the hypnotist as a super human, super powerful and super evil monster, combined to give hypnosis a "bad name." Somehow it became associated with stage shows, charlatanism, and quackery which became most damaging for professionals.

The recent resurgence of interest in and use of hypnosis by professionals today has been stimulated by proofs of effectiveness, improved techniques, and the development of understanding of some of the psychophysical and psychodynamic laws underlying the hypnotic process.

Most of all, perhaps, the increased educational level of the public has dispelled many mystical notions about hypnosis and the vague supernatural fears that used to be so prevalent. A more sophisticated and intelligent populace is looking for real answers to today's "civilization-produced problems," and are seeking deeper and more reasonable philosophies of life so that they can be whole, complete and at peace with their physical and mental being.

I read Dr. Van Warrebey's book with great interest and

pleasure. It is in harmony with these deeper philosophical needs, which go hand in hand with practical methods of application and lead to the emergence of peace and harmony within the person. There is a current T.V. ad for a news magazine which says in effect, *"ours is a serious publication - we save our readers from unimportant news - and we save our advertisers from unimportant readers.* Dr. Van Warrebey's book is similar - it is not meant for the non-serious reader. The book is not a cookbook for a quickie cure for the superficial person. The book is a profound thoughtful and sensitive philosophical exposition of society today given with care, insight and compassion. Simultaneously, it offers a basis for real answers from within each individual and then produces the method of achieving the peace, harmony, confidence, success and self-esteem that he seeks.

Although no book can provide all the answers for all the readers, I was especially impressed that Dr. Van Warrebey has made provision for answering the reader's questions on a personal basis, in addition to providing an excellent bibliography of readily available references.

While written for the layman, I do feel this book to be a must for every professional as well.

Jay Sanford, M.A.
Licensed Psychologist
and Marriage Counselor

A FOREWORD FROM A DENTIST

With the recent upsurge of clinical hypnosis within the scientific community, a truly informative source book for all levels of readers is imperative. This text is sure to receive due recognition because of its new and pertinent approach to the philosophy of hypnosis. As a composite of philosophical ideas, and a concrete guide to hypnosis, it results in a new conceptual rationale for clinical hypnotism and for self improvement. Drawing upon his experiences and clinical expertise, the author has been able to coordinate the basic principles of hypnosis with the world around us. Rather than just present a step by step guide to hypnotic procedures, he has successfully integrated it with personal experiences from everyday life, which results in making learning not only easier but enjoyable for the reader.

After envisioning a new philosophy of approach, the individual can extract segments which are applicable to himself and his daily life. If the reader will open his mind to incorporate some or all of the philosophy, he will become a better person and will derive the most from this text.

The author has a commanding use of language and has included a broad range of disciplines. Dividing his work into two major categories, he gives the reader a chance to develop his own acumen on the philosophy of hypnosis and P.H.S. and then a chance to adopt and use it for his self improvement. The writer conceptually coordinates various aspects of life in such a way as to result in an orderly approach to self and others.

Never condemning peoples' actions, but rather constantly advising a way of self improvement, this book is an invaluable guide to self knowledge. The author not only has a keen insight into the problems of people but he has a true compassion for their problems. He offers a solution which most people can develop and follow.

This text has become a valuable asset to my own personal and professional library. It has already been reread several times, and will surely be used again and again in the future. Each time I read it something new becomes relevant and applicable to myself and my perception of those around me. I am sure that all readers, from the novice to the clinical expert, will derive both pleasure and knowledge from this book, coming away with a new insight into this field and themselves.

J. Phillip Kurtz, D.M.D.
Member of The American
Society of Clinical Hypnosis
and The International Society
of Clinical and Experimental
Hypnosis

"New opinions are always suspected and usually are always opposed, without any other reason, but because they are not already common."

- John Locke

"It is not the things which happen to you that upset you, it's your view of these things that upsets you."

- Albert Ellis

OVERVIEW

Part 1

MISCONCEPTIONS: AN ADJUNCT

This segment of the book can be utilized as a supplement or an adjunct, for those readers who have little or no background knowledge of hypnotism and hypnotherapy. It will direct its attention toward the common myths, fallacies and misconceptions of hypnosis, and objectively attempt to re-educate the reader about them. Those people who have an elementary conception of hypnotism may journey directly to the introduction.

First of all, there is absolutely nothing mystical about hypnosis. It is a proven and often tremendously effective science. However, it is neither a panacea nor a cure-all.

In 1958, hypnosis was formally accepted by the American Medical Association. Each year it becomes more popular within the realms of psychiatry, psychology, medicine, dentistry and other professional areas. Many uneducated patients, however, still view hypnosis with self-defeating skepticism and fear. They have preconceived ideas about hypnosis based upon such quasi-authorities as hearsay, stage hypnotists and mass media fiction (for example, stories on television and radio, in movies and in books). Also, man has classically feared the unknown, and what he does not understand often is a direct result of his own ignorance.

There is nothing to be afraid of in hypnosis, since the ultimate source of hypnotic power is within yourself! Hence, all hypnosis is self-hypnosis. This is more obvious in self-induced hypnosis, but it is also true in other-induced hetero-hypnosis, such as hypnotherapy, where the hypnotherapist acts only as a catalyst. In analogy, he is only the rudder and you are the sails and boat. If you are receptive and trust and believe in him, you will open your sails (mind) to the natural God-given wind and current of hypnosis. When this occurs, you will go much deeper and the desired results may be accomplished more easily.

People often ask: "Just what is hypnosis?" Hypnosis is an altered state of consciousness, which is characterized by an exaggerated "open-mindedness" or positive suggestibility. In hypnotherapy, this open-mindedness can be extended into a therapeutic suggestibility. Thus, defenses and resistances to certain suggestions which "normally" may be present are often obviated.

Under hypnosis, a person will never do anything morally or ethically against his or her character. Neither can persons be hypnotized against their will. Also, a person is always able to come out of hypnosis whenever he or she wishes to, though, it should be said, most people enjoy the profoundly relaxed feeling and going with the suggestions so much that they stay "in" until the session is completed.

Another question that often arises is: "Can anyone be hypnotized?" The answer is yes, in approximately 97% of the cases. Every day, we all fall into some form of light hypnosis—many authorities consider daydreaming and hypnosis to be synonymous (Fross, 1965). Even though our society fosters a kind of defensive "closed minded-ness" in most individuals, we can get in contact with our "natural openmindedness" (positive or therapeutic suggestibility) when we enter and become engulfed in the hypnotic state. The intelligence of an individual really does not matter. If the person cooperates, results are normally excellent; if a person resists, results can be minimal. Whether one has "weak will" or a "strong will," the ability to concentrate and relax will increase the probability of success.

Freud made the analogy that the mind is like an iceberg...a small part is above water (conscious) and the larger part is below (subconscious). Some authorities (Adams, 1976) claim that self-hypnosis can revive the 92 per cent of potential mental power that is unused in the average man. Adams claims that a successful man is not possessed by power, but rather that he controls and possesses the power within himself!

A person will not tell any secrets while in hypnosis, unless he wants to, nor will he be "asleep" (as we usually use the word). Basically, the person in hypnosis is in a state of consciousness, halfway between the normal sleeping state and the awakened state. For example, in hetero-hypnosis, one must hear and follow directions and suggestions (from the hypnotherapist), therefore he is not "asleep". However, the words "sleep" and "asleep" are used by therapists because they are easily associated with and can produce extremely deep relaxation. Semantics are critically important in hypnosis - imagine what would happen if a hypnotist or hypnotherapist said to a new client, "Let yourself drift into a somnambulistic trance." Instead, he may say, "Let yourself drift down as if you were deep asleep."

Again, contrary to what we see on television, etc., most people are aware of almost everything occurring while they are in hypnosis. Once in a while, new patients will say; "I'm not sure I was hypnotized." Their preconceptions, based upon the previously mentioned false authorities, throw them a curve ball. The author finds the expectations of some patients to be quite amazing, if not altogether magical.

The person in hypnosis is always aware of background noises and of his or her environment. This is normal. William Reardon, M.D. (1965) notes that it has been said that one's awareness is increased one thousand percent in hypnosis. He states that eighty-five percent of the work done in hypnosis is done in the light to medium hypnotic state.

SECTION I

Introduction

    This book involves itself with a rather basic, yet effectively innovative, approach to self-hypnosis. It should be mentioned, however, that Part 1 will be theoretical in orientation as opposed to the more applied ''Method'' section of Part 2. Because of the Method's comparatively simplistic nature, one can gain a commonsensical working knowledge of self-hypnosis within a relatively short period of time. For best results, it is strongly advised that the reader send for the author's record album or cassette tape, ''Hypnosis for Self-Improvement and Actualizing Your Potential.'' (See the last page of this book for more information concerning this recording.)

    Unlike most books on self-hypnosis, this book will stress aspects of suggestion formulation rather than trance or hypnosis induction. This is done because it's assumed that the reader either: 1.) is utilizing the above mentioned recording, which includes a comprehensive hypnotic session and leaves only the (self-improvement) post-hypnotic suggestions to be formulated (These suggestions are ''tailored'' to the individual's needs by himself, presumably with the help of this text.); or 2.) has a background in self-hypnosis but needs further knowledge of suggestion formulation; or 3.) is able to attain adequate trance depth by the procedures and reference delineated herein; or 4.) any workable combination of the above three.

    Within the context of this book, the author wishes to establish an approach to self-hypnosis based upon: 1.) practical experience and what has proven to be effective in his private practice, and 2.) an integration of current trends and theories with hypothesis formulation. Also, as the title implies, careful attention will be devoted to the proper formulation, development and placement of post-hypnotic suggestions. The main reason for this is that in much of the related material on the market today, sections dealing with post-hypnotic suggestions are frequently underemphasized, unclear and/or too esoteric for the layman. Secondly, though the previously mentioned recording places the subject (one who is being hypnotized) into a state conducive for posthypnotic suggestions to work, the lay subject may not be sure as to when or how to place the suggestion.

Using the vehicle of post-hypnotic suggestion, the entire hypnotic phenomenon is contoured to the subject's individual needs and/or problems. Within these pages, steps will be taken to assist the subject in all matters involving post-hypnotic suggestions.*

Since the large majority of self-hypnosis books address themselves to Western and, hence, often common and cursory approaches to the subject, this book will take a more holistic viewpoint, based on the need for a cross-cultural thesis. At the least, we need to recognize other cultural viewpoints and relative similarities. This approach may, indeed, expand our conception of self-hypnosis, demonstrating its universality in principle and supplementing other literature which is, at least to some degree, a result of cultural bias.

In keeping the context of this book in the realm of simplicity, the complementary cross-cultural sources will be largely taken from Zen Buddhism and Taoism. A second aspect of the book which is conducive to a holistic conception is its theoretically eclectic perspective.

*Many subjects can gain invaluable assistance from a hypnosis consultant. Hypnosis consultation and hetero-hypnosis should be done by a competent hypnotherapist, psychologist or physician with credible training in hypnotherapy. If you wish, you may write The American Professional Hypnosis Association, P.O. Box 7, Sparta, New Jersey 07871 for information concerning the whereabouts of hypnosis consultants in your area.

WHAT IS A POST-HYPNOTIC SUGGESTION?

A post-hypnotic suggestion (P.H.S.) is a suggestion which is placed in the subject's subconscious mind, either by himself (self-or auto-hypnosis) or by another (hetero-hypnosis). This stimulates defined actions or responses which fulfill themselves after the hypnotic trance. They are defined or re-defined by the subject in auto-hypnosis and by another in hetero-hypnosis. In reviewing the literature available to the layman, the author was amazed to find so many books on self-hypnosis and hypnosis which did not clearly and lucidly define the term "post-hypnotic suggestion." Ostensibly, the reader was to be already acquainted with the basic concepts of hypnosis when he began reading these books. The writer believes that the function of P.H.S. is the core of auto- and hetero-hypnosis.

When a subject comes out of hypnosis (is dehypnotized) and manifests these previously defined actions or responses, he is said to be reacting to a post-hypnotic suggestion. For example, when a stage hypnotist says to his subject, "When you awaken, you will have a terrible itch on your left foot and you will have to scratch it..." and the subject scratches it minutes after being in hypnosis, he is reacting to a P.H.S.

Though less ridiculous and more therapeutic, the phenomenon is similar when an individual enters the author's office wishing to stop smoking through hypnosis. While under hypnosis, the subject may be given suggestions such as "from now on, you are in control of your behavior, you are a nonsmoker." Weeks later, the author may telephone the individual to find that, following the P.H.S., he has not smoked.

In order to achieve ultimate success with hypnosis, one should combine auto and hetero-hypnosis. Hence, in the above-mentioned case, the smoker may be told, both in and out of hetero-hypnosis, that he will continue with autohypnosis at least once a day for several weeks. During this time, he will be deepening his trance and reinforcing and strengthening the hetero-P.H.S.

SECTION II

Hypnosis and Belief:

A Social, Psychological and Philosophical Approach

In a time of rapid technological, sociological and psychological change, it has become increasingly clear that a critical problem has evolved for Western Man which affects him and his society with growing amounts of alienation, dehumanization, maladjustment and insecurity. Unlike our ancestors and the older members of our society, we no longer can obtain much security from traditional "social absolutes" (Colemen, 1976). Institutions, credos and values that were internalized for hundreds, even thousands of years, like the traditional close family, social law, religion, politics, education, sex roles etc., no longer "seem" viable. (see Appendix II).

Modern Western Man is wrapped up in a frustrating, pragmatic, bureaucratic and synthetic world in which it becomes harder to adjust with each passing day. Apparently, he believes in little beyond worldy possessions, and has even less to hold on to. In a nebulous world of vacillating belief, real security seems imperceptible and unattainable. In short, Western Man is progressively losing his faith in the ultimate structure and foundation of his seemingly chaotic environment. This environment undoubtedly reflects a part of him, and this may become pathogenic.

Belief is obviously a crucial factor! Man needs to truly believe, especially in himself, as well as in his environment. Otherwise, he will not know who, what or where he is. Eventually, this could lead to some rather bizarre and schizoid consequences, both for the individual and his society. Without true belief, man becomes disoriented and dehumanized!

Why is *true belief* dwindling and often hard to establish? We have mentioned the modern phenomenon of the deterioration of social absolutes. This is a notable part of the problem.* Giving direction and even impetus to this is the second aspect, the age-old phenomenon of "charlatanism".

The results of 20th-century charlatanism are compounded by the mass media. For instance, Richard Nixon surely had a deleterious effect upon people's belief and trust in the political institutions of the United States. How about the scandals and "rip offs" we read about every day in the newspapers? Even worse, look at the everyday prostitution of social law. What does it mean when the often sycophantic lawyer takes his client for a painful and overly expensive ride? To add to this, he is supervised by a past master of parasitic virtues, the sometimes pseudo-omniscient/omnipotent judge who interprets social law in a world of increasing relativity, contradiction and disbelief. The judge, with his projective inverted inferiority complex, his soapbox stage and captive audience, behaves as if he had a deep-seated need for attention and to "act out" which throughout his life was suppressed, repressed and unfulfilled. Like his lawyer peers, he is an "intelligent" though terribly frustrated actor.

Meanwhile, the castrated taxpayer and the apathetic middle-class sit by, "turning the other cheek" and repressing their hostility!

What most people do not understand is that presidents, lawyers, judges, doctors and the like are role models. Unfortunately they are, in many cases, schizoid and sociopathic role models. Ironically, the ethnic and lower classes, in many instances, are modeling after and copying these disjointed role models, doing their own "rip-off" (example: the 1977 "black out" in New York City). They understandably rationalize this behavior by pointing to the sick system. However, when they get caught, they get "burnt" (punished) whereas the socially elite most often avoid punishment. The difference between the educated sociopathic role model whore and the ghetto thief seems to be merely I.Q. This is another source of conflict and disbelief among the different classes.

*Conversely, there are also good points to the "deterioration of social absolutes" that we must consider (example: redefining the role and meaning of human sexuality.)

In the world of psychology and hypnotherapy this aspect is spearheaded by what might be called "Hollywood Therapies". Bookstores, magazine articles, ads and even interviews on radio and television are saturated with "how-to" books, questionable guarantees, fads, pseudo-movie-star therapists and the like. They seem to have one thing in common which has great appeal to the often lazy Western Man: "If you buy our product, you will quickly gain this or that (whatever you want)!" Naive Western Man is often ready to pay money for a magical cure-all, even though he many times acknowledges that he does not "believe" in them. But money is neither going to buy a cure-all, nor be the cause of a spontaneous recovery. To achieve self-mastery, one must invest in himself not economically, but psychologically, philosophically and spiritually. He must have true belief!

We now arrive at a point where we must make a psychological delineation, one which finds its roots in a classical philosophical argument between Pierce and Descartes, concerning doubt. For time's sake, we will not go into the lengthy context of the argument, but rather, begin with the notion of belief and the hypothesized polarity of it.

There seems to be two kinds of belief, true belief and feigned (or false) belief. We are all acquainted with them both, to some extent. Feigned belief can frequently be recognized as a profane verbal and often conscious phenomenon, which usually is a result of, or is assisted by, the ego defense mechanisms. Presumably, the subconscious is usually detached from this belief. Thus, in feigned belief, there is a cleavage between cognition and behavior (thinking and doing). This is an important point and it may, indeed, have further ramifications within the realms of psychology (as in the behavior/mentalism controversy). Thus, within this frame of reference, when a person says to himself, "I am going to..." and days or weeks later does *not* do what he or she set out to do, we might consider this individual to be operating with a feigned belief.

On the other hand, in the case of true belief, cognition and behavior are, in a sense, one and the same. Conscious and subconscious belief are integrated. When one says to himself, "I'm going to..." and he *does,* he has true belief.

Unquestionably, many philosophers and psychologists would agree that man has an innate need for true belief.

Though our society has, in many ways, diminished, prostituted and profaned true belief, self-hypnosis offers a viable alternative; a way to reinstate this age-old aspect of man in Man.

I.T., WILL AND EMOTIONALIZED IMAGINATION

> For man, mind is the cause
> of bondage and mind is the
> cause of liberation....[1]
> Bhagavad-Gita

To attain true belief, which is necessary for the best results in hypnosis and self-hypnosis, one must have Internal Triumph (I.T.) over disbelief. This is gained by coordinating the conscious mind to work in harmony with the subconscious. To understand this more fully, we can look into the operations of the conscious and subconscious.

Earlier, an example was made of a stage hypnotist who told his subject that when he awoke, he would have an itch on his left foot. When the subject followed this P.H.S., he demonstrated the subconscious acceptance of a suggestion. Thus, in hypnosis, the subconscious accepts suggestions uncritically--it believes indiscriminately. The conscious mind which normally determines what is real and unreal is circumvented.

If the subconscious mind reasons at all, it reasons only deductively, whereas the conscious reasons both deductively and inductively. Invariably, in a test of strength, subconscious beliefs outweigh conscious beliefs. Basically, subconscious beliefs are in a way more "real" to the individual, though they may be unrecognized, adaptive or maladaptive, right or wrong, even fact or fiction.

It is the opinion of the writer that the reason why the subconscious is stronger is because it has "flexible nonsense." In the case of the subconscious mind, the central active element of "nonsense" seems to be an emotionalized imagination. This emotionalized imagination, being a function of nonsense, is rather pliant and supple as compared to its structured counterpart in the conscious mind, will.

Will, being a conscious phenomenon, is restricted because it must strive to make sense. Conscious phenomena are dictated by social norms, logic and linearity. Imagination is flexible and less structured.

A conflict becomes apparent when, as often happens, the subconscious mind believes one thing and the conscious mind believes quite another. At this time, the defense mechanisms come to the rescue. The rescue, paradoxically, in most cases is "adaptively maladaptive". For instance, if an individual wishes to lose weight and consciously wills himself to stop eating junk food, a conflict is imminent. Imagining how it would gratify him, this person is tempted to, for instance, eat candy. Though he may fight this temptation for a while, the defense mechanism(s) allows him to break down and eat in a fashion which is "adaptively maladaptive".

It is adaptive because he no longer suffers through the anguish (conflict) which presents itself when his will and imagination clash. It is maladaptive because he can not consciously control his behavior. Rationalization and denial are common defense mechanisms in such conflicts. The following are typical examples: Rationalization — "I'll eat the candy now, but tomorrow I will exercise and stick by my diet." Denial — "It does not bother me that I am chubby."

In this light, we may endeavor to add to the earlier quote from the Bhagavad-Gita. For man, the conflict between will and imagination is his bondage and the harmony of will and imagination is the cause of his liberation. What is necessary is to educate the subconscious. We will continue with this notion later on.

I.T. over disbelief is attained when the subconscious and conscious beliefs are integrated. One must utilize his will and imagination in harmony. At this point, he *truly believes*....Oneness and homeostasis exist.

TWO WAYS OF VIEWING THE WORLD

According to the ancient Chinese writings of both Taoism and Confucianism, the perfect man or sage is in

Yin and Yang harmony. For such intuitively wise people, Yin and Yang is a universal concept which explains the very basis of life's force and that which is. If Yang is male, Yin is female. When one is hot, the other is cold. They are "harmoniously opposite," relative to each other, and the mid-point between the two is called the Middle Way (synonymous with the ancient Greek concept of the "Golden Mean").

In his innovative work, Ornstein (1972) maintains that the cerebral cortex of the brain is divided into two hemispheres joined together by a bundle of interconnecting fibers called the corpus callosum. Ornstein's hypothesis, backed up by considerable resources and research, is that both the structure and function of the hemispheres underlie two modes of consciousness. He maintains that the left hemisphere is basically involved with verbal and mathematical functions and uses analytical and logical thinking. On the other hand, the right hemisphere is more holistic, creative and relational. Where the left hemisphere is more sequential in its mode of operation, the right hemisphere is simultaneous.

We can see an interesting Yin and Yang here which could possibly be extrapolated to parallel the hemispheres of the earth. That is, we in the West (Yang) seem to be more mathematical, verbal, analytical and logical (in terms of Platonic dualism and Aristotelian logic). Conversely, in the pre or non-technological East (Yin), people seem to be more intuitive and holistic.

Earlier, Erich Fromm (1962) referred to a fundamental difference in religious attitudes between the East and the West. In actuality, this distinction goes much further than religious attitudes. He expresses this difference in terms of logical concepts which find their roots, in the West, with Aristotle and with what we would consider to be logical (example: A cannot be A and non-A). Juxtaposed to the Western concept of logic is a kind of "alogic" which Fromm calls "paradoxical logic." This would, for example, maintain that A and non-A do not exclude one another.

Thus, for our use here, a paradox is something that, at first, may seem self-contradictory, but is really true and valid. For example, "We are all the same and not the same." Where Aristotle and Plato would claim that this statement is invalid, an Eastern philosophy such as Taoism or Zen would claim its validity.

Aristotle said, "It is impossible for the same thing at the same time to belong and not to belong to the same thing..." [2] The ancient Chinese philosopher Chuang-Tzu maintains: "That which is one is one. That which is not one, is also one." [3]

Thus, it seems we have two diametrically opposed ways of viewing the world. The hypotheses which I propose are: 1.) Alogic and/or paradoxical logic are valid ways of explaining things that do not fit into the Aristotelian framework and 2.) the conscious mind, in some respects, "fits into" the Aristotelian paradigm and the functions of the left hemisphere (i.e., logical, analytical, verbal, sequential, etc.) and the subconscious mind, in ways, fits into the paradoxical framework and the right hemisphere (i.e., holistic, artistic, relational, even simultaneous, etc.).

BALANCING OUR CONSCIOUSNESS

> And when you have reached
> the mountain top, then you
> shall begin to climb.
>
> Kahlil Gibran

As was implied in the last section, we in the West are, at best, using only half of our brain. We are using the verbal, mathematical, linear, analytic side. But how much of the other side are we using? How many people do you know who are truly artistic and intuitive, not to mention being creative or imaginative in their approach to life? How does one develop his right hemisphere? In what ways does a developed right hemisphere enhance self-hypnosis? These questions will now be addressed.

It would seem that very few people in our culture fully utilize the potential of their whole brain. Because of our system of education (especially "higher education") there are not many individuals who are artistic, intuitive or creatively imaginative. In the West, the romantic archetypal artist is being replaced by a kind of confused neo-robot. Our society inhibits the artist and the individual intuitive type and reinforces the automatic, scientific and analytical type.

How many artists work for the government? In what way does the government stimulate imagination, intuition and creativity in the armed services or even among government workers? Relative to the automatic, scientific and analytical type of person, how many artistic or intuitive people "make it"? And what does "making it" mean here in the West as contrasted to the East?

This book does not espouse the concept that one should use only his right hemisphere, but rather, an appropriate balancing of the two. Thus, this position is in contrast to both the Eastern and Western views. This appropriate balance will not be accomplished by an over-emphasis on intuition and paradoxical logic, such as can be seen in Zen and Taoist philosophy. Neither will it be accomplished by the excessive use of analytical logic used by almost all Western philosophers and people in our culture.

Einstein is a classic example of an individual who had integrated the artist intuitive type with the analytical scientific type. He would not have accomplished what he did, if not for this balancing! He holistically integrated both hemispheres with a kind of Middle Way conception/perception of Art and Science.

SECTION III

The Beginning Concepts and Procedure

What is it you wish to truly believe? Possibly, you may wish to truly believe that you no longer desire cigarettes and that they actually taste bad! Perhaps you would like to truly believe that you are relaxed and have more conscious control of your behavior. How about truly believing that you gain more self-confidence and conscious control over your emotions with each passing day?

Obviously, there is a large assortment of things one can work on. Using self-hypnosis, one can effectively integrate the conscious and subconscious beliefs. Hence, when this complementarity is established, self-mastery is an important result. In the following pages, we will discuss certain concepts and procedures which make this possible.

DEVELOPING THE RIGHT HEMISPHERE AND OPEN-MINDEDNESS

> The submissive and weak will
> overcome the hard and strong.
>
> - Tao Te Ching 3,500 B. C.

It is presupposed that the reader has an adequately developed verbal, analytical, mathematical, and linear repertoire (left hemisphere). Thus, we shall endeavor to investigate the notion of how to utilize and develop the right hemisphere for self-hypnosis.

First, we will review the paradox of strength and its relationship to consciousness. The above quotation is a fine one to keep in mind.

Strength and control are obviously important factors in hypnosis and self-hypnosis. Often, because of the ''nonsense'' element of the subconscious, one controls behavior by *working with* a paradox. This is because the subconscious, not confined to the Aristotelian kind of logic, has *flexible nonsense* which may derive its impetus from the *emotionalized imagination.*

As was observed earlier, this flexible emotionalized imagination and nonsense of the subconscious is always stronger than will (its counterpart in the conscious). It is more durable, since emotionalized imagination will always triumph over the constricted logic of will. This is true just as water "wears down the stone" and the "weak overcome the strong."

This phenomenon is clearly exemplified in the Law of Reversed Effect. The Law states that the more you consciously try to do something, (eg., change a habit) the less chance you will have of succeeding. Ironically, according to this Law, you actually strengthen the idea or habit that was to be changed. "Making" or "trying" imply conflict! You should "allow" something to happen. This can happen paradoxically, by aligning your weak imagination (which is strong) with you strong will (which is weak). Now, both your conscious and subconscious can be focused to combat a given task or problem.

Throughout Taoist and Zen philosophy, one is continually reminded that in order to master a problem, one must passively "give way" and transcend verbal analytical thinking (the left hemisphere and Aristotelian logic). When a psychiatrist asked a Zen Master how he dealt with neurotic people, he replied, "I trap them!" "And just how do you trap them?" said the psychiatrist. "I get them where they can't ask any more questions!" [4]

It is this same method that the Master of Judo uses, since the philosophy of "The Gentle Way" finds its roots in Taoism and Zen. The Master of Judo overcomes the strong (problem) by becoming "actively passive," by becoming, in one sense, weak. In this way, he uses his opponent's strength or "resistance" to his advantage.

Like Zen Buddhist and Taoist meditation, self-hypnosis clears the mind by concentration and relaxation. You can not *make* this happen, as you will encounter resistance. One must *allow* it to happen and it does! The mind must become "actively passive" and receptive.

Throughout the literature related to hypnotism, writers stress the importance of suggestibility. Kroger and Fezler (1976) maintain that: "Suggestibility refers to a suggested act that is uncritically carried out without the individual's logical processes participating in the response." Logical analysis is transcended. Suggestibility is a primary element in the development of hypnosis. Thus, in hypnosis, one is not "asleep" in the traditional sense, but he is "creatively imaginative" and "actively passive," which stimulates positive suggestibility.

The Zen of hypnosis is the transcendence of the analytical/defensive (left hemispherical) modality, which "gives way" to the intuitive/receptive (right hemispherical) mode. When the subject comes out of hypnosis, disengaging the right hemispherical mode, he again utilizes the left hemispherical mode. It is the degree to which one can appropriately and effectively control these transitions that will indicate one's ultimate self-mastery...the Homeostasis of consciousness. It is a known fact in the field of hypnotheraphy that the analytical and intellectualizing individual has a noticeably slower symptom remission than does the suggestible patient. Hence, to gain the most out of the therapeutic hour, suggestibility is an asset.

Many of us in the West have developed a negative attitude toward suggestibility. We think of it as a "weak" aspect of the individual. Ironically, we confuse strength with weakness!

For this reason, the author wishes to expand upon his concept of *selective open-mindedness.* In the past, clients have asked him questions like, "If I go into hypnosis now, will it make me more susceptible to radio and television advertising?" Or, "Now that I have gone into hypnosis with you, does this mean that I can go into hypnosis at any time, or be hypnotized by anyone?"

The answer is no, because most careful hypnotherapists will, while the client is under hypnosis, always suggest that, for instance: "You will be susceptible to hypnotic suggestions and go into hypnosis only when I say deep asleep." Thus, only the patient's hypnotherapist can automatically put him or her in hypnosis. In this same way, self hypnosis can be more "selective" with regard to open mindedness or suggestibility.

Obviously, there is a need for a concept of "selective open-mindedness," which actually is "positive suggestibility" put in different words to avoid the connotation of naive ignorance. Selective open-mindedness can and should be increased, in the same way the classic concept of suggestibility develops into hyper-suggestibility. From now on, as the book continues, the concept of selective open-mindedness will replace the concept of suggestibility. The key distinction between the two, in a therapeutic sense, is the *creatively imaginative* component of the former as opposed to the implicit gullibility of the latter.

EXISTENTIAL (SELECTIVE) AUTOMATISM AND DEAUTOMATISM

In a very real sense, what hypnotherapy seeks to achieve is what may be called *selective automatism and deautomatism.* The author's concept of existential or selective automatism and deautomatism is a humanistic conception of cybernetics as applied to psychology. Writers in the field of psychology have discoursed upon the need for deautomatism in our complex "robot-like" society. While this is certainly true in many circumstances, there is also a real need for automatism in others. For example, a very basic need for the human being is self-preservation. The ultimate in "open hand" self-defense, be it karate, judo or boxing, is the automatic response. The master of his martial art reacts almost reflexively and automatically, which, in this case, is certainly adaptive and necessary. The Zen perspective combines awareness with the automatic response.

Beginning with an insight or awareness of its need, selective automatism is accomplished when a desired response or behavior happens automatically. In the same way, selective deautomatism occurs when an undesirable response is slowed down or stopped. A problem arises when, as is often the case, a negative response or behavior occurs or continues without awareness.

When removing a fear, habit or emotional problem, selective automatism and deautomatism complement each other in the way they accomplish a single task. For instance, if one is aware of a snake phobia, the hypnotic prescription could include an automatic relaxation response when presented with a snake stimulus and a suggested deautomatism of the previous response pattern or fear.

If one chooses to curtail his or her intake of alcoholic beverages, the process is similar. For instance, in hypnosis, a person may accept the suggestion to automatically increase his relaxation response via P.H.S., substituting natural relaxation for the pseudo-relaxing effects of alcohol. At the same time, it could be suggested that an increased awareness and deautomatism of his undesirable behavior will occur. The phenomenon is similar to, and gathers some direction from, the counter-conditioning techniques developed by Wolpe, 1969. (See "reciprocal inhibition" and "systematic desensitization.")

In a discussion which entertains a seemingly "mechanistic" notion of automatism and deautomatism, several theoretical and philosophical points should be taken into consideration. At birth, for example, human beings are by nature random action creatures. As they develop, they become less random and more structured. *This structuring is a kind of automatism, that is, basically a result of external manipulation and/or choice.*

As a human being, one is entitled to, and deserves to choose, options which directly affect one's self and one's future. This is especially true if the results of choosing do not hinder any other person and are, to a relative extent, in harmony with society's norms. In the case of external manipulation by society, one may choose to learn from the experience. In an analogy, this is making medicine from poison. In any event, to "flow with" and accept a certain amount of manipulation is to change its form—resistance is transmuted to work for the individual. This is certainly not to say that anyone should passively and apathetically accept gross manipulation. That is foolish. Maslow maintains that the insecure person is preoccupied with seeking acceptance, as he adjusts to and goes with the insane society, attempting to gain acceptance. On the other hand, the self-actualized individual can actively disagree with society (McMahon, 1977). We must concede to the fact, however, that we are a part of a larger whole, whose being is our ebb and flood. Without constriction, we surely would not know freedom. Our freedom of choice is a pleasure and a human need.

The automatism stimulated by external manipulation or coercion is often dehumanizing and robot-like (mechanical). On the other hand, the automatism stimulated by choice (selectiveness) is more humanistic and non-robot-like. The former is a result of what Freud might have called an "overbearing culture," whereas the latter is a result of self-knowledge and freedom of choice. This dichotomy may at first appear to be rather simple, though with further investigation it proves to be a valid conception.

It should be noted that deautomatism is robot-like if it occurs because of a breakdown in a system or systems of man. On the other hand, if it occurs because of an existential awareness or a therapeutic insight, it can more appropriately be viewed as a humanistic phenomenon because it implies a choice has been made.

One of the central precepts of Zen is that true knowledge comes from within, it is "intrinsic." In Za Zen meditation (which is analogous to the altered states of consciousness in hypnosis), one pursues knowledge and enlightenment. "Extrinsic" knowledge from institutions, books, etc. is secondary, if not totally superfluous. (See Appendix II for an inquiry into the notion of the ultimate strength of intrinsic vs extrinsic reward).

Existential knowing and automatism are intricately interwoven. This can be seen in the Gentle Way. One needs to know (self-knowledge) to have the automatism work for, not against himself. A common "pathology of the average" is an inappropriate automatism or habit that, at one time, was appropriate. In this case, the automatism is the symptom, which exists usually because of a combination of faulty knowing and denial.

As has been inferred, there would seem to be two corresponding types of knowledge and automatism that emerge in each individual. The first is a result of choice or personal "selectivity." It is intrinsic, more long lasting and humanistically harmonious. This knowledge is a result of insight and freedom of choice, though realistically it too can be, and often is, subject to influences and impressions from the external world. The automatism that arises from awareness, insight and freedom of choice is a humanistic or existential automatism. It is most definitely not robot-like, because it is explicitly a function of awareness, insight and freedom of choice. A robot has neither insight, nor freedom of choice.

This brings up an important point. The reader may question why the author uses the concepts of automatism and deautomatism when, seemingly, he could have used the "conditioning" (*ergo* Skinner) framework for elaboration. In contrast to the "insight" and "choice" elements of existential automatism and deautomatism, the conditioning paradigm is mechanical and dehumanizing. The meaning of the experimentalist's "reproducible results" is also often questionable (Schulman et al, 1976). Contrary to the behavioristic model, results attained from rats, apes and college "volunteers" are, by far, not representative of a "human population!" The strict behavioral conditioning viewpoint is a sick conceptualization and ultimately produces an abominable neurosis in the society afflicted with it.

Once again, the second type of automatism is robot-like, because it is mechanistically dehumanizing and a function of external manipulation. This "robot knowledge" is extrinsically acquired, and is likened to the Skinnerian view of conditioning. It implies a conflict between one's individualism/humanness and the manipulating external world. It is this profane and erroneous perspective that pervades behaviorism proper. B.F. Skinner's downfall will be largely attributable to this conception of the essential nature of Man. He will probably go down in history as being a brilliant man who either was ridiculously inflexible or lost his capacity for common sense. He gets paid well (extrinsic reward) for taking such an ass's stand!

Man is more than an organism, he is a "humanistic" being who, with certain (not all-pervading) constraints, can to a substantial extent choose his destiny.

Let us look at existential knowledge and existential automatism/deautomatism. They denote the individual's humanness in harmony and in the process of actualization. Whereas existential knowledge (a kind of "Zen knowing") revolves around and utilizes awareness and insight, "robotism," because of its conflict basis, most often stimulates aggression and repression. The human choice notion along with the "Computer Child" concept (of Section VI) integrates the "mechanisms" of man with his ultimate humanism. This is a holistic view, a "Middle Way" conception, which reflects two very real aspects of the human being.

In another sense, whether one's theoretical perspective (bias) is more mechanistic or humanistic is really not important. What is important is that there are many knowledgeable people supporting different poles of the same proposition. It seems reasonable to believe that in a way, they are both right to some extent. Thus, to again quote Chuang Tzu: "That which is one is one. That which is not one, is also one." [3]

Once again, it is far easier to choose from an assortment of options than to be forced into one. However, sometimes we simply do not have that much choice. We all have relative, different and changing amounts of freedom of choice. As human beings, we should utilize our harmonious existential knowledge and existential automatism/deautomatism to its fullest potential. The master of judo *puts himself in a position* of maximum flexibility and choice. In this way he throws the external manipulation. In the situations and times of less choice, we must be aware of and especially work with the manipulation of the external world. In a way, we can use its strength against itself, by fully accepting and knowing it. This is a Judo of the epicurian conflicting harmony between the individual and his society!

Man is free most of the time if he sees himself this way. Though at times he may feel his freedom constricted, he then must knowingly be aware of, work with and accept it, as this is an exercise of existential humanism and an act of true knowledge. These factors expand one's freedom of choice and foster a flourishing humanistic quality of being. However, to "not know" and to deny or repress the manipulation and yet "work with it" is to be a robot. To knowingly or unknowingly oppose it is clearly foolish.

COOPERATIVE AWARENESS OR COMPETITION?

The one person who had, perhaps, the greatest impact upon the realms of psychology was Charles Darwin, best known for his book, *The Origin of The Species.* Essentially, this book concluded that man evolved from a more primitive organism. He also maintained that the types of organisms which survived from generation to generation were ones that had characteristics which enabled them to cope with their environment. These characteristics were passed on to their offspring.

Research psychologists, both comparative and general experimental, compose the majority in the field of psychology. In a sense, they owe their professional existence to Darwin, since each accepts, and bases his assumptions upon, the premise that man evolved from a lower organism. Ergo, the results of Pavlov's and Skinner's research on animals (i.e., dogs, rats, etc.) have been extended and extrapolated into their conceptions of the human being. (The author believes this extension is in some ways questionable. Man is more complex than the lower animals. However, we will not go into this notion right now.)

The notion which is critically important to bring out at this point is Darwin's overemphasis on nature's conflict and competition and his underemphasis on the harmony and cooperation in nature. He was only half right! This, however, was not fully Darwin's fault. As with other great thinkers, Darwin's logical-conceptual apparatus was stongly determined by the social and psychological influences of his environment. Moreover, as we discussed earlier, we, as well as Darwin, are indirectly though profoundly influenced by Platonic dualism and the logical principles of Aristotle. In contrast, the Eastern concept is more flexible and harmonic. Hence, for instance, an Eastern philosopher never argues!

The conflict pervading our view of the world is dramatically exemplified in Western sports and in Western education, which have competition as their ultimate ideology and philosophy. Viewing the world and reality as being in competition and conflict is "normal" in the West. This is crazy!

Physical and mental education are a polarity in the West. "Never the twain shall meet." Conversely, in Eastern philosophies such as Zen or Taoism, the mind-body is viewed in complement as One. This is quite a contrast to Platonic dualism and the consequences of operation in this pathogenic modality.

Where Western philosophy and, to a great extent psychology center around antithesis and divergence (eg. argument and problem finding), Eastern "psycho-philosophy" revolves around synthesis and convergence. (eg. meditation).

Psycho-philosophical sports such as Judo, Aidido and TaiChi are prime examples of a cooperative approach to life in action. This cooperative element of Eastern philosophy in action and in thought becomes a Way of Life. It is thus immutable rather than transient like the effects of conflict-oriented Western psychotherapy (for example, psychoanalysis and behavior modification).

The mammoth mistake that we make in the West, which spans from our political philosophy to the way we shine our shoes, is that we can not concede the fact that as much can be attained with cooperation as can be attained with competition. This concept has been used productively in some of the Communistic countries.

The author believes that the reason people have so many problems in positively therapeutically changing themselves is because they self-defeatingly define what they are doing or wish to do in a complex and/or conflicting manner. This is also a problem for people who have difficulty reaching adequate trance depth. This complex and/or conflicting definition is a result of an internalized, irrational belief that change must occur with great difficulty! It is vividly seen and demonstrated every day in the internalization of the work ethic. Though he is often not aware of it, the subject in hetero-hypnosis is "conditioned" to compete with the hypnotherapist, rather than cooperate with him. The person in many cases "subconsciously" defines what the therapist is doing as a game or threat. Hence, the therapist must reeducate this person and redefine what he is doing.

If one meditates or contemplates and becomes "aware" (in the West, this is surely an enlightenment in itself), he will find that he can achieve as much with a cooperative attitude as he can with a competitive one. It is so simple! By becoming more cooperative one at the same time transcends resistance.... *Resistance continues and causes habits and ailments!*

It is this aspect of Cooperative Awareness which enables one to achieve self-mastery. The individual learns to flow with that which is. Thus, the reader has been offered another alternative that he may choose to take. He will find that it is good to view the world in a way which helps him better himself.

MILIEU INTERIEUR AND ENVIRONMENTAL FACTORS

The crucial physicochemical relationship between the extracellular fluids and the internal conditions of receptor cells (or sensors) is referred to as a milieu interieur. We can extrapolate this homeostatic concept into the critical psychosociological relation between the environment (or milieu) and the internal conditions (primarily psychological) of the individual. As in the physicochemical relations, if there is a "toxin" or noxious element in the environment the intricate psycho-sociological homeostasis is disrupted. As in the case of Yin and Yang, there is an interaction—one effects the other and vice versa.

Homeostasis implies a balancing and congruence. When homeostasis is disrupted, the balancing and congruity is disrupted. At this point in the system, be it physicochemical or psycho-sociological, a *compensation* occurs, reviving homeostatic balance. When this compensation occurs physicochemically scientists consider it a normal and desirable phenomenon. However, when viewed through the eyes of psychology proper, compensation carries with it a certain connotation of psychopathology — it is in this instance seen as an unconscious (though sometimes conscious) defense mechanism, where the individual attempts to make up for a real or imagined, psychological and/or physical deficiency.

There is a diversity of environmental factors which varies from individual to individual. Also, we all respond to the same stimulus in (often slightly) different ways. The important point with respect to hypnosis, is that some people live in an environment which is so noxious that it actually is a deterrent to the fruition of their P.H.S. In fact, the stress, anxiety and frustration in one's environment, in many cases, substantially accounts for the presenting problem.

Pathological compensation emerges sometimes in a symbolic form. The author is reminded of a newspaper editor who came in for therapy to help him quit smoking.

The man was overtly nervous, tense and had a notable obsessive-compulsive tendency. The nexus of his problem seemed to center around his inability to relax. Between the stress and anxiety of operating the newspaper and marriage problems at home, he was in quite a bind. He was smoking three packs a day on the average. The cigarette was a psychological compensation.

In his own words, he explained that his cigarette smoking compensated to a degree, for the environmental confusion and lack of sexual gratification. The oral (aggressive) symbolism became more obvious as he elaborated upon his environment and how he viewed its effect on him. As the session progressed, the patient conceded that in order to totally quit smoking (without symptom substitution) his environment would have to be altered considerably. His attitude became more realistic when he accepted the fact that hypnosis was not going to "magically cure" his sick environment. It was suggested that he either get a less stress-related job, or consistently indulge in progressive relaxation intermittently at work (during breaks, lunch time, etc.) and self-hypnosis with relaxation as a P.H.S. at home. It was also recommended that he and his wife begin seeing a marriage counselor.

During a follow-up investigation six months later, Mr. "X" informed the author that he had not quit smoking. However, he had cut down from three to less than a pack a day. The client noted that he was "cutting down step by step." He concluded by stating that his marriage and related sexual difficulty were resolving, and that he had delegated a considerable amount of responsibility to his junior administrators, which he previously kept to himself.

THE CONFLICT BETWEEN ID AND SUPER-EGO

According to Freud, there are three parts to the "psychic apparatus." They are the id, ego and super-ego. Freud maintained that the id is unconscious and contains the energy which comes from the instinctual drives and desires of the individual. Opposed to this is the super-ego which is also largely unconscious. The super-ego develops from: 1.) the internalization of the ethical standards of one's society and 2.) by identification with the attitudes of one's parents. When investigating *some* presenting problems it is often helpful to view them through the psychoanalytic framework.

The following is a brief overview of a comparatively common case of orgasmic dysfunction in a twenty-six-year-old female. The attractive, college educated female visited the author's office wondering if hypnosis or self-hypnosis could help. After a lengthy verbal interview, it was found that Miss "Y" had never had an orgasm while in the act of coitus. However, she admitted that she was easily able to have an orgasm by auto-erotic masturbation. Thus, it was understood that she had a secondary dysfunction (Masters and Johnson) and that the prognosis was good.

Miss "Y" had several sexual/emotional affairs (over 15) previous to her current boyfriend. She had a "normal" upbringing, though she was still notably dependent on her father at the time of intervention. One may assume from a modified psycho-analytical perspective that her id was operational, as exemplified by the number of affairs she had. However, it would seem that her sex life was dominated by the unconscious manifestations of her super-ego. Of course, there were other variables in concurrent operation that we will not go into for the sake of time and simplicity.

The hypnotic/self-hypnotic implementation was relatively simplistic and effective. First, we must give credence to the fact that with each "failure" she compounded and to some degree self-fulfilled the dysfunction. Secondly, the client disclosed that she had in the past, during intercourse, tried to "make" an orgasm happen, rather than "letting" it happen. There was a classical conflict between what she consciously wanted to happen and what was actually happening subconsciously. Hence, she was working against the Law of Reversed Effect. Thirdly, she noted certain unresolved emotional pain associated with some of her past lovers. This emotional pain was coupled with a less conscious distrust of males (not including her present boyfriend).

The boyfriend came into the office the next day and could be characterized as being caring, attentive, cooperative and receptive. It was suggested to the boyfriend that he allow a greater amount of time to be devoted to foreplay (for example, 20 minutes instead of the usual 3-4 minutes). He was encouraged to manually stimulate her in a way very similar to her own auto-erotic technique. These things were to be done directly after her self-hypnotic session, where she utilized erotic visual imagery with a P.H.S. for deep relaxation and erotic pleasure. The two were instructed to consistently continue this motif each and every time they engaged in coitus.

Miss "Y" was seen for several weeks thereafter, as she kept the author informed of her noticeable progress. In this time, she was developing her trance conditioning, as well as resolving the repressed emotional pain via hypnotic abreaction and revivification. She began to develop a quite therapeutic "let it be" attitude which seemed to become more and more accepted and internalized by the subconscious. Ostensibly, the super-ego was lessening its grip and within two and one half weeks, she had her first orgasm while in the coital act.

In the following sessions she began to talk about and "work through" her distrust of males and the over-dependecy on her father. Presently, she enjoys a wholesome and functional sexual relationship with her boyfriend.

This case demonstrates the effectiveness of a hetero-hypnotic and self-hypnotic therapeutic intervention. It also reveals the strength of the unconscious and the basic dynamics of the id and super-ego. The understanding of and *working with* the Law of Reversed Effect is also of primary importance.

METHOD

Part 2

SECTION IV

AN INTRODUCTION TO P.H.S. FORMULATION

Once again, the focus of this book addresses itself to the proper formulation, preparation, development and placing of post-hypnotic suggestions (P.H.S.). Again, the reader is advised to use the aforementioned record album (see last page), which brings the subject into hypnosis leaving only the "tailoring" of the situation-specific (personalized) P.H.S.(s) to be developed by himself. As a supplement or alternative to this, the reader may refer to the enclosed bibliography or write for a free mail-order book list to: The American Professional Hypnosis Association, P.O. Box 7, Sparta, NJ 07871.

Arons, an author in the field of hypnotism, notes that most of his students want exact formulation of the particular P.H.S. applicable in any given case. However, he believes that an individual will gain more by using his own imagination and inventiveness. This is an important fact! In addition, we are paradoxically "all the same and not the same" and a prescription filled by a pharmacist under the direction of a physician is only an approximation. Hence, as with an individual's reaction to drugs, there are different and occasionally divergent reactions to the same suggestion in hypnosis.

Personal and individual semantics are extremely important in hypnosis, as is body chemistry in pharmacology. When developing a P.H.S., one must consider the exact meaning of the words that make up the P.H.S. Remember, the subconscious accepts suggestions from their literal meanings.

Likewise, *we all have a different order of precedence when listing problem causes as well as goals*. A problem like obesity may have any number of causes or interacting variables. In terms of goals, one person may want prestige above all else, another may desire love or money. In hypnotherapy, an individual's goals or motivation stimulus or stimuli can be used to change a behavior, habit or even to redefine and eventually resolve a problem cause (see Appendix II, re. extrinsic/intrinsic reward).

Though this text will elaborate upon "basic" P.H.S.'s

and their exact verbalizations, one must concede the fact that it is only an approximation aimed at the mean or "average" member of society. There are three small problems: 1) no one is the exact mean or average; 2) precise causes of a given problem vary (to some degree) from person to person and have a different order of precedence, importance and meaning with each; and 3) the exact verbalizations herein represent a blanketing rather than focused effect.

The generality of the section (VIII) dealing with exact verbalizations may have the less desirable result of resolving the "symptom" but not the "cause." In this case, there is a greater possibility of symptom substitution. It is for this reason that tailoring and personalizing the P.H.S.(s) beyond the enclosed "exact verbalization" section, utilizing other relative concepts and notions included herein and in the bibliography is suggested. *The exact verbalization should be viewed as a point of extrapolation and personalization.*

Let us look at an example to which reference was made a little earlier. There are many reasons why people become obese. The causes may range from a strictly organic pathology, like a thyroid dysfunction, to a purely emotional and/or psychological one. We must be sure not to rule out multiple causality.

It may be noted that many medical doctors attribute 70-90% of the problems presented by their patients to an emotional and/or psychological cause. The author has found, in an abundance of cases, that problems often arise from multiple and interacting causes. Independent of this, the order of priority for causes seems a function of individual differences. It is always advisable to consult with an authority, unless one is absolutely sure that he knows the cause and can adequately cope with it.

In the case of obesity, one person's basic problem (or pathology) may be that of, in analogy, "eating his frustrations and anxiety." Another's may be quite different. One individual may have a residual sexual problem, another's pathology may be only partially sexual, or another's, not sexual at all. Obviously, we could go into a considerable amount of complexity, but this is not the focus of this book. In the final analysis, the combination of self-knowledge and receptivity to suggestion is the preferred phenomenon which leads way to the desired result.

Basically, if the cause is not resolved, you may reconcile the symptom possibly only temporarily and have it transformed into another (symptom substitution). The question is, is the substitute better, worse or just as bad? Thus, the classic problem arises when quitting smoking: "Will I gain weight?" (a negative and possibly "just as bad" symptom substitution). It is a practice of the author, in this case, to transform the symptom (in the first session) into a "better" substitution until the cause is found. When this happens, then steps are taken towards its eventual neutralization or reconciliation. Thus, in hetero-hypnosis, the subject may be told, if he wishes to quit smoking: "You will derive as much (oral) satisfaction by sucking on toothpicks" (acceptable substitution). Or the person with the weight problem may be told: "Diet foods, vegetables and protein foods taste great! You will become increasingly aware that you enjoy them more than fat garbage food."

As intra-psychic therapy (for example, psychoanalysis) is known to be longer in duration when compared to behavioral therapy, resolving the cause most often takes more time than treating the symptom. This is rather important and should be kept in mind when doing self-hypnosis. The author suggests a regime, which includes a "here-now" change in behavior and symptom with a more long-term step resolution of the causality. In the case of several causes, the subject may begin with the resolution of the "lesser evil," progressively graduating to the most complex, or hardest to change.

In terms of the self-help approach to cause resolution, the individual must objectively determine what is the etiology of the problem. He then subjectively investigates what things would significantly change this: motivation stimulus, goals, etc. Lastly, he should integrate the above knowledge (self-knowledge) in a way that changes attitude and behavior positively, with least resistance.

The first step is to change behavior, which may imply symptom substitution. The second and more dynamic step would include a progressive "intra-psychic" reconciliation and attitude change accompanied by the desired behavior. Hypothetically, paralleling the ''progressive'' intra-psychic reconciliation or autogenic neutralization of problem cause, the ''need'' for the symptom and substitute symptom diminishes. In this case, both symptom and cause are resolved.

SECTION V

TAO, RESISTANCE AND SELF-KNOWLEDGE

> The Tao (Way) in its course does
> nothing and in so doing there is nothing
> it does not do.
>
> - *Tao Te Ching* 3,500 B.C.

To the ancient Chinese "Tao" literally meant "Way" or "law." They believed, as do our contemporary scientists, that everything has a Law or Way. Scientific investigation is a study of the way or Tao of whatever science or art is to be studied. To know its Way (Tao) is to know it. For the psychologist or hypnotherapist, the "psyche" is that which is studied. The "psyche" has its Way (Tao) and the "psyche scientist" must study its Tao to know it.

From Lao Tzu to William James through today, the mind or psyche has been simply likened to a stream or river. The ancient Greek philosopher Heraclitus averred; "you can not step twice into the same stream," for it is in constant change. James poetically used the phrase "stream of consciousness." Thus, as individuals or groups, we are the same and not the same as we were the day before.

In change there is almost an implied resistance. Thus water, which is most supple, finds its course in the *Way (Tao) of least resistance.* "Least resistance" (maybe the slow but progressive wearing down of the riverbed stones) is still resistance. Though there are many Ways or theoretical perspectives to produce therapeutic change, the Way of least resistance is the ideal. This ideal, however, is real and viable.

In Section IV, a causal approach was developed. Basically, it was established that: 1) Positive behavioral change is to be implemented immediately even if the symptom is transformed into a less innocuous one, and 2) in time, cause is to be found and reconciled. To give a more global viewpoint, we must also give consideration to another theoretical perspective. The renowned Alfred Adler, in his conception of Individual Psychology, stresses and focuses on the goal or final method rather than the "causal" method. He sees the individual as a unity and all his life manifestations are directed toward his life goal. Thus, where, in analogy, Freud saw the individual "running away" from X (eg. repression) Adler would see the individual "going toward" X (eg. goal). Thus, to view ourselves more globally for self-knowledge, we may look at both causes and goals.

It is important at this point to touch on the notion of *emotional need for symptoms.* This is another variable that deserves consideration, for many patients are not aware of it. The hypochondriac is not the only one who exaggerates the profoundness of his problem, which in most cases is purely psychological.

For instance, there can be a deep-seated need to manipulate others for personal gain. Possibly, it can also be a neurotic need to affect others and gain attention by means of the symptom. These people are often like children and, if they can not "get their own way" or gain attention positively, they will get it negatively. Masked behind the symptom, "insulated" from retaliation, the individual can maladaptively have his or her emotional needs pathologically satisfied. Kroger (1976) states:

> Some of the commonest of these are the need to inadvertently exaggerate the severity of their complaints as a means of getting more attention, to avoid responsibilities of marriage or parenthood, to dominate their home environment in a neurotic manner in order to compensate for their complete inability to deal with their problems in a realistic and mature manner and finally, to use symptoms as a means of self-punishment for guilty fears."[5]

Duckworth (1976) "generally" concludes that in every case of illness, there are two factors: "One is purely physical, the other is moral or imaginative."[6]

In gaining self-knowledge (awareness), one must objectively perceive himself, for a moment, as if he were a *sensitively analyzing other.* At the same time, he can objectively determine if this perception is the same as his subjective (or introspective) one. If it is not (which is usual), then one can "review what is" and analyze the subjective/objective cleavage. After this review and analysis, the individual can take steps toward the integration of this knowledge with the formulation of his particular P.H.S.

We must concede the fact that this "left hemispherical" approach has its drawbacks, in that there really is no such thing as a purely "objective" perception of self by self. However, it is a close approximation, which is satisfactory for a P.H.S. to be effective. Of course, one could supplement this with professional analysis and hypnotherapy.

In changing one's concepts and perceptions of himself, his situation, or his problem, one may take a course of least resistance. "Let it happen" is indeed a prescription and a therapeutic attitude. As we alluded to earlier, "making it happen" indicates force and conflict. Remember, *the course of least resistance implies that the will goes with the imagination.* They must complement each other for progressive change. Like the master of Judo, he gives no resistance to his opponent, but in effect allows him to throw himself. If his opponent pushes, he pulls; if the opposition pulls, the master pushes. Conflict is transcended, convergent synthesis occurs. *Cooperate and throw your problem!*

In gaining self-knowledge for one's P.H.S. formulation, the individual investigates what things work for him. He seeks to discover what will ensure the desired behavior and the complementarity of his will and imagination.

A PARADOXICAL APPROACH TO REALIZING AND ACCEPTING CHANGE

In an excellent essay, *The Paradoxical Theory of Change,* Veisser appropriately asserts that "Change occurs when one becomes what he is, not when he tries to become what he is not." [7]

A novice once asked a Zen master, "How do I find Zen?" The master replied, "You are Zen!" In an analogous case, the writer (who also has a black belt in Judo and Karate) once had a conversation with a student of martial arts from a distant school. The student explained that years back he had observed one of his fellow students talking to his master instructor. It was a Sunday, and his school (Dojo) was open for practice seven days a week. The student was explaining to the Master that he thought he should go to church rather than work out all morning in the Dojo. The master replied, "You are in church always."

What both of these masters were trying to convey to the new student was that: *You are there, you just have to realize it!* Contrary to the bumper stickers and signs saying "I found it," they should say, "I never lost it and I am realizing it!" You have to be a part of it to really find it! Too many of us in the West experience life's profundity as part-time observers, rather than as full-time participants!

The Zen or Gestalt approach to hypnosis might be to have the individual become *aware* and *realize,* that in a sense, he is there and he has achieved the goal! Resistance might be seen, in part, as a malady which develops from the sick Western social norms of goal chasing and game playing. The Zen perspective transcends the conflicts of opposition and dialectics. There is nothing to do! There is no Buddha to worship!

Thus, when Veisser notes that "Change occurs when one becomes what he is, not when he tries to become what he is not," he is saying the same thing as the Zen master. When you *realize* and *accept* that "you are Zen," there is nothing else to do... you are there! The goal is a "goalless goal," the goal is an extension of yourself.

In hypnotherapy, for example, when the patient "truly believes," realizes, and accepts that he is a non-smoker, he is! When he truly believes, realizes and accepts that he has self-confidence, he has. Relax, there is no conflict. This is a profound meta-scientific approach. It is a "satori" (literally translated from Zen Buddhism: "one's own enlightenment"). From this moment on, you have achieved your goal and you are "getting better and better with each passing day!" Time only reinforces and internalizes this!

Ironically, this approach is often too "simple" for the Western Mind. As observed previously, people in the West seem to subconsciously strive toward a more difficult route, a way of more resistance. They mistakenly believe that in achieving anything, conflict must be present, and that the more conflict that is endured in accomplishing the objective, the more "worth" is attached to the objective if and when it is accomplished! It is this frame of reference that discourages them from changing in the first place! *I.T. is simple, do not make it difficult!*

SECTION VI

THE "COMPUTER CHILD" CONCEPT AND THE LAWS
OF HYPNOSIS

RELAXATION AND THE COMPUTER CHILD

Modern Western Man in his frustration/anxiety-ridden technological world can do so much, but ask him to relax and he may find that he is incapable of this "simply profound" task.

The ability to relax is a key facet in the development of hypnosis. In hypnosis, relaxation and concentration assist each other, as hypnotic analgesia and anesthesia used in dentistry and medicine has shown. Fross (1966) maintains that the pain threshold can be raised in direct proportion to the relaxation of the subject's musculature. Paralleling this is the interesting work being done with autosuggestion, within the realms of biofeedback. Natural childbirth (Lamaze method and/or the strictly "hypnotic" approach) is another area which is similar, if not synonymous.

We can also consider the meditating religious sub-culture of monks in Japan who walk bare-footed over a bed of red hot coals once a year. Here we have concentration, relaxation and success-oriented thinking which produces a focused anesthesia.

When one is relaxed, his or her "defenses are down" and what we will call the *computer child* is for a moment exposed and unguarded. In this moment of exposure and unguardedness, one's computer child in the subconscious can be humanly programmed in a passively active manner.

Just what is the computer child concept? Maxwell Maltz, M.D. in his fine book *Psycho-Cybernetics* likens the subconscious mind to a "computer." (Others have likened it to a tape recorder.) Basically, he maintains that if the subconscious mind is "programmed" correctly, it will achieve the results that one wishes. However, it is believed that this strictly "mechanistic" notion should be taken a step further. The use of the word *child* denotes a certain humanistic aspect. *Computer* seems to be a far too mechanistic classification even when used in analogy. There are far too many psychological, as well as philosophical "flaws" in the strictly mechanistic concept. We are not machines, we are humans with certain psychophysiological mechanisms.

We could briefly make note of certain salient intrapsychic schools of thought, to validate the "child" aspect of the "computer child" theoretical cross-fertilization. Where Rank would talk about a subconscious need to return to the womb, Freud would talk of the ever-present subconscious child in everyone. According to Freud, the individual has a subconscious wish to return to infancy. Therapists who use transactional analysis have a similar parallel in their analyzing of the individual in terms of adult, parent and *child.*

All hypnotherapists are aware of the fact that subjects respond best to simple or picture words. During hypnotic age regressions, the fetal position is often observed; in fact several of the author's patients assume the fetal position from the moment they make contact with the office couch. The child is suggestible and interprets reality as defined by parents and adults (authority figures).

During maturation, what Freud would call the "super-ego" takes over as a kind of inner authority reflecting society's norms. Ostensibly, our society constructs and suppresses the child by making him "defensive" in response to society's manipulation. The conscious adult is subconsciously defensive. In hypnosis, the "depth" and degree to which the computer child is receptive, seem contingent upon how creatively imaginative or how open-minded it is.

The computer child is obedient if programmed right and disobedient if not. It remembers all input from all five senses. The computer child and its "unguarded moments" could be likened to what Coue called, the "outcropping of the unconscious."

People have different thresholds of defensivenss (Yang) and open-mindedness (Yin). This is, at least in part, a function of "social Darwinism." However, relaxation enables the defense threshold to be lowered and exposes the computer child to suggestions and impressions. Some subjects who have difficulty attaining adequate trance depth may find that the problem is not the induction method but the inability to fully relax due to their own subconscious defensiveness, which may be partially hereditary, though it would seem to be largely a "learned response."

Past impressions, possibly of a threatening nature, elicit a defensive response. When this response is repeated over and over, it becomes ingrained and internalized. Hence men, being the "protectors" and "defenders" in our society, are sometimes not as relaxed and as good as subjects as are women. A man's defense system is "stonger" (keep in mind the paradox of strength).

In this light, one could conceptualize the rationale for the P.H.S. as being a counteracting measure against the effect of undesirable past suggestions and impressions. There is a need for educating and/or re-educating the subconscious, specifically the defense system. The person must learn to truly believe and utilize the selective element of open-mindedness. Repetition and increased relaxation will ensure the occurrence of open-mindedness in hypnosis.

If the subject maintains his "libidinal position," that is, if he resists the change from adult/defensive to child/open-minded, depth and therapeutic effect will be lessened. It is true that it is hard to be relaxed when defensive, but it is also true that it is hard, if not impossible, to be defensive when relaxed. The two juxtaposed responses are incompatible and cannot take place concurrently.

We must conclude from this that relaxation is absolutely necessary in hypnosis. Moreover, when one increases his "relaxation response," he at the same time becomes less defensive and increases his probability of success. Now, he can choose to humanly program his "computer child" in a way that will ensure the desired existential automatism/deautomatism.

THE LAW OF REVERSED EFFECT

By seeking to increase something it
often decreases and by seeking to decrease
something it often increases.
                    - Tao Te Ching, 3,500 B.C.

As the ancient Chinese had conceptualized the law of relativity in their concept of Yin and Yang over four thousand years ago, so too were they aware of The Law of Reversed Effect. This paradoxical concept is common throughout the writings of Zen and Taoism, as the above quotation from Lao Tzu's *Tao Te Ching* exemplifies quite vividly.

This Law was a late but still remarkable discovery for Western Man. Essentially, as originated by Coue in the West, it states that the harder one endeavors (wills) to change or do something, the less likely it is that he will succeed. Moreover, in "willing" oneself to do or accomplish something, you will strengthen the resistance to change.

For instance, the more you "will" yourself to perform sexually, stop smoking, get over emotional pain, sleep, remember, etc., the less chance you will have in succeeding. This is one of the main reasons why people who start self-hypnosis without a good background fail. For best results one must know and work with the laws of hypnosis.

The resistance factor (will vs. imagination) is a key issue. Duckworth uses the word "effort" rather than "effect" in his excellent explanation:

> Now the term voluntary suggestion also carries with it the implication that an effort is being made to do something--that there is an obstacle to be overcome. We are, therefore, thinking of two things at the same time--the desired end and the effort we are expending to accomplish it. Thus, there is conflict. And if the notion of effort is the stronger, there will probably be a negative result. By the law of reversed effort, the thing desired is denied. [8]

When there is no effort, there is nothing to oppose. The target is a "target-less target," an extension of the subject who is (metaphorically), a projectile in actualizing flight.

Coue's law of reversed effect is analogous to Kano's principle of "maximum efficiency with minimum effort." Maximum efficiency with minimum effort is achieved by "giving way." When opposition comes, the Judo master *goes with it,* like a tumbleweed rolls ahead of the wind. Opposition turns into harmony - he throws it! So too can a bad habit or a presenting problem be thrown.

Where the Zenist and Taoist uses Wu-Wei (non-striving), Wu-Hsin (without mind) and Wu-Nien (without blocking or choice) and meditation, Coue eliminates conflict and opposition by the education of the "outcropping of the unconscious." This is done with psycho-physiological relaxation and positive suggestions that *work with* will and imagination. [9] When the mind is tranquil and at ease (not defensive), it is, at the same time, "effortlessly receptive" to suggestion.

THE LAW OF CONCENTRATED ATTENTION

> Isan said to his disciple,
> Gyosan, "all day you and I
> were talking Zen. What did
> we accomplish after all?" [10]

The Law of Concentrated Attention states that the more concentration and exposure (repetition) one has to an idea, the more it will become internalized. Kroger and Fezler (1976) maintain, "Whenever attention is concentrated on an idea over and over again, it spontaneously tends to realize itself!" The repetition aspect of The Law of Concentrated Attention and the "passively active" programming of The Law of Reversed Effect make a very effective combination.

The mass media utilize The Law of Concentrated Attention every day, as we are bombarded with advertisements on radio, television, etc. Many use catchy tunes appealing to a "captive audience" ...a short time passes and, lo and behold, after enough repetition (media saturation), we may find ourselves not only buying the product but humming the tune! Why else is "Coke" a household word?

Coue concluded, with regard to indirect exposure,

that one idea begets another idea. Perhaps we can once again look at the mass media for our illustration. At any time you can look in a magazine or at television and see a pretty young woman advertising a product. She becomes "associated" with the product. The males who look at the ad may say to themselves: "I (would) like her," while females may think: "I wish I had her..." (figure, hair, eyes, etc.). Previous to the ad stimulus, there was no "I like her" or "I wish I had her" effect. Thus, the ad stimulus has produced a desire or an idea of possible pleasure or satisfaction, which then sparks some degree of emotion/imaginative reaction.

The model, while drinking a can of Coke, stimulates the original idea of desire and may engage another idea - to have a Coke. She may also be pictured in the hot sun or doing something which may cause her to perspire (the observer is lead to assume). Hence, another idea begets another idea - thirst.

With repeated exposure, the idea becomes firmly planted in the subconscious. This is done most often without the use of overt persuasion, which may cause a reversed effect. Most people buy Coke (and most other products) by the label alone. They are conditioned by media saturation. In this same way, our *computer child* can be negatively programmed. We can see the necessity for "selective" open-mindedness which comes from self-knowledge and awareness.

The Law of Concentrated Attention also works in more therapeutic ways. Let us take a standard suggestion hypnotists use: "Every day in every way, you're getting better and better." Now, if a person used this suggestion over and over in self-hypnosis (maybe 20-30 times a day for a month), he would accordingly notice a subjective difference in the way he felt about himself - "better and better."

The subconscious computer child progressively self-fulfills the suggestion. People's subconscious defenses are lowered with repetition and relaxation. They become more susceptible to suggestions, more open-minded. If additional situation-specific (personalized) suggestions are made, the individual can repeat and concentrate on these in the same way. Remember, relaxation is an important factor. With repetition and relaxed (passively active) concentration, the suggestions and idea become more and more internalized and part of the person's subconscious reality.

THE LAW OF MENTAL HABIT OR AUTOMATIC RESPONSE

The Law of Mental Habit or Automatic Response (M.H.A.R.) is very similar to The Law of Concentrated Attention. Where the Law of Concentrated Attention begins the automatism process, the Law of M.H.A.R. internalizes it, makes it automatic and in effect, "visceral knowledge." Thus, in self-hypnosis, when one "consciously" starts a desired change utilizing The Law of Concentrated Attention, this change will become a desirable "habit and/or automatic response," by means of repetition. Selective automatism/deautomatism is essential.

Though P.H.S.'s sometimes have a temporary effect (for example, if the symptom is resolved but not the cause) they also have a cumulative effect. Thus, once again we come back to the need for repetition of P.H.S.'s, leading to the desired automatism and deautomatism.

P.H.S. repetition should continue at least until the desired response or effect is obtained (i.e., using the Law of Concentrated Attention). Even at this point, one should go into hypnosis periodically and repeat the P.H.S., therefore internalizing the subconscious reality of the M.H.A.R. In other words, the undesirable habit, behavior or effect is becoming deautomatized while the desirable habit, behavior or effect becomes automatized.

Dumont (1976), in a nicely put metaphor and explanation says:

"It costs less trouble to fold a paper when it has been folded already. This saving of trouble is due to the essential nature of the habit, which brings it about that to reproduce the effect, a less amount of the outward cause is required.... Just so, the impressions of outer objects fashion for themselves in the nervous system more and more appropriate paths, and these vital phenomena recur under similar excitements from without, when they have beem interrupted a certain time...so nothing is easier than to imagine how, when a current once has traversed a path, it should traverse it more readily still a second time." [11]

THE LAW OF ROLE PLAYING

Western culture is above all a role playing society. This law utilizes this "neurotic" cultural norm to facilitate a therapeutic change. The Law of Role Playing uses the basic tenets of the laws of Mental Habit or Automatic Response and of Concentrated Attention. Once again, the end product is selective automatism and deautomatism.

The Law of Role Playing utilizes the "as if" principle. That is, one may role play "as if" the desired change had already occurred. As time passes, the subject finds that he is role playing less and that the desired attitude and behavior is progressively more and more a part of his reality. Thus, conscious programming of the "computer child" gives way to the desired subconscious automatism and deautomatism, and the role actually becomes integrated into the personality matrix. (See "magical thinking" in Appendix I).

From the very first moment after a self-hypnosis session, the subject should consider the change to have already taken place! No longer is there a distinction between what one "wants to occur" and what is occurring. In analogy, the goal is "touched" and now it is progressively assimilated and digested. In accordance with Veisser's Paradoxical Theory of Change, the subject "has become what he is."

Repetition of the actualizing role over time produces the "mental habit" or the "automatic response." Relaxation and actively passive repetition that works with The Law of Reversed Effect eradicates resistance "day by day in every way." The new self-image is established. In hypnosis, visualizing oneself doing all the fantastic things that this (desired) role offers is also a helpful and motivating force. In hypnosis, one should note that he or she is completely relaxed and comfortable with the new role.

One assumes a role commensurate with the goal to be achieved. The new role may range from that of a very "confident" individual, to a "satisfied and relaxed" person. If one wishes to quit smoking, one "plays the role" of a nonsmoker!

THE LAW OF ANTICIPATED JUDGEMENT

Paul Adams (1976), in his instructive book *The New Self-Hypnosis* explains:

> One of the powerful forces in motivating men is that of anticipated judgement.... If you don't do right, you will be judged at the Great Judgement Day.... One of the oldest gimmicks for motivating people is the future promise. If you work a little harder, I will give you a raise someday, etc. The individual who responds to this does so because he believes that sometime in the future he will be rewarded. [12]

When one expects to be judged, there is an implicit reward or punishment. This principle has been used quite successfully for thousands of years by Western religions. In fact, almost every religion, including Christian Science, uses principles of hypnosis and self-hypnosis (Fross, 1974).

For an example, if a person were in the Navy and had gained fifteen unwanted pounds since the last time he was "stateside," he could use the Law of Anticipated Judgement to lose the weight. (Notice here that several of the Laws come into play, interweaving to produce the desired result.) Specifically, let us assume that this person is on a nuclear submarine in the middle of a 60-day underwater voyage. In thirty days he will be in port at New London, Connecticut, so his self-hypnotic "deadline" date for losing the weight is in thirty days. The sailor anticipates his girlfriend to be waiting for him at the pier, and in an indirect but very real way, he is anticipating her judgement of himself.

He may imagine that a (voiced) negative *judgement* by her would be a kind of covert punishment. Alternatively, a (vocalized) positive *judgement* by her would be a covert reward.

To achieve his goal, he could automatize his behavior in one way (automatic fully satisfied relaxation) and deautomatize it in another (decreased impulsive eating). By anticipating and imagining the extrinsic rewards (loving, sharing, kissing, hugging, coitus, etc.) of losing the weight, motivation is sparked and the goal is easily accomplished. Imagination works for him.

To facilitate this, it is good to develop a symbolic mental image which will act as a "reminder/motivator" which keeps the goal uppermost in one's mind. For instance, before and during exercise or eating, the sailor might imagine his girlfriend in some erotic position and make an image of this. For him, this would serve as a strong "reminder/motivator." Once again, we all have a different order of extrinsic motivators, although emotional or sexual ones most often work best (see the Law of Dominant Effect).

The important thing is to develop a here/now approach with a *realistic deadline.* In the above case, the sailor could "allow himself" to lose some four pounds a week for a month (30 days).

Similar in many ways to the Law of Anticipated Judgement, the Law of Self-Approval maintains that "other-approval" stimulates "self-approval." This also acts as a motivator which can be utilized in obtaining a desired result. We must remember that this is an operant conditioning approach (ie. extrinsic reward) and can manifest less lasting results. For instance, when the reward is received, will the person continue the reward-seeking behavior? (See Appendix II).

THE LAW OF DOMINANT EFFECT

Probably one of the most effective laws of hypnosis and hypnotic therapy is the Law of Dominant Effect, or what Adams (1976) calls the "Law of Positive Dominant Emotional Motivator." The central point of this law is that a stronger emotion has a tendency to replace a weaker one. Emotions are intrinsic, though they can be stimulated extrinsically or intrinsically.

Maslow's hierarchical Need Theory suggests that everyone has needs that range from self-preservation to self-actualization. Self-preservation, being the strongest need, is more important or more necessary than is self-actualization. Self-actualization is, therefore, contingent upon self-preservation. Likewise, we each have a hierarchy of emotions and emotional motivators. Unlike Maslow's theory, which implies that the need hierarchy is the same for everyone, actually our hierarchy of emotions seems to be more individualized or personalized. For one, love is emotionally most gratifying and for another money is above all else. In a third case, an individual may find "status" most emotionally satisfying.

This is where subjective introspection is important. To utilize this law, one should construct a personal hierarchy of emotional motivators ranging from the weakest to the most powerful. The critically important ones to find are those which are strongest.

In elaborating upon the Law of the Positive Dominant Emotional Motivator (P.D.E.M.), Adams assures us that:

> "Feelings," the result of emotions, are the prime movers among human beings. Advertisers are well aware of this fact. Very seldom do they make an appeal to the intellect - their appeal is always to the emotions...If you wish to improve a particular aspect of your life, or change a habit, or overcome a hindrance, you must find a dominant emotional motivator which will be stronger than the emotion which now dominates you...regardless of the situation, always emotionalize your self-hypnosis with your P.D.E.M. [13]

In the first part of this book, we briefly discussed the role of emotionalized imagination. In self-hypnosis, it is the proper use of your emotionalized imagination and its positive dominant motivator that will result in the fulfillment of your goal(s).

In a demonstration of how these laws overlap, the reader is asked to recall the last law discussed. An example was made of a sailor who lost weight using the Law of Anticipated Judgement. To increase the effectiveness of his P.H.S., he combined the Law of Dominant Effect with the Law of Anticipated Judgement. Hence, in addition to using the "anticipated judgement" of his girlfriend as a motivator (reward), he used a personalized P.D.E.M., in his case the erotic "reminder/motivation" image.

The sailor could have developed his ''reminder/ motivation image'' to prompt him to eat less and to do an extra 30% more exercise. Being on such a long and ''celibate'' voyage, in hypnosis he could visualize his girlfriend and himself at the desired weight (15 pounds less) running nude on a beautiful long beach. He could also suggest to himself that he will let himself lose this weight and he will be running on the beach with his girl the day after he gets in (deadline). He could also visualize her ''praising'' him for his physique and muscle tone, as this would also be a conducive human motivator.

Here we have the ''anticipated judgement'' and ''deadline'' of the Law of Anticipated Judgement. From the Law of Dominant Effect, we have the P.D.E.M., which in this case would be sexual excitement (sublimated into physical exercise) as a sexual/emotional motivator. This is just an example of how to personalize your P.D.E.M. It is imperative to gain self-knowledge and awareness of one's P.D.E.M. Again, this can be done with subjective introspection and self-study, from which one can determine just what feelings and emotions would best motivate him or her to achieve the goal.

THE LAW OF POSITIVE AND SUCCESS-ORIENTED THINKING (IDEATION) AND CONSISTENCY

As we have previously discussed, central to the science of hypnotism and hypnotic therapeutics is the notion of positive success-oriented ideation. One's ''consistency'' is also an important factor. When positive and success-oriented thinking are combined with consistency, repetition and relaxation, profound results are achieved - the ''computer child'' becomes properly and humanly programmed! There is no doubt that this method works - we need only to look at the many successful people in our society who directly attribute their success to ''positive thinking.''

The best advice is to *continue this consistent positive and success-oriented thinking both in an out of hypnosis.* Whether at home, work, play or in hypnosis, remember to think in a manner which is consistently positive! Promise yourself that if a negative thought enters your mind, it will automatically be replaced with a stronger positive one.

You can also make a personalized positive and success-oriented post-hypnotic formula and memorize it word for word. In the event something negative happens or enters your mind, tell yourself that you will consistently repeat the hypnotic formula over and over (eg. twenty times).

SECTION VII

MAKING YOUR PERSONALIZED POST-HYPNOTIC FORMULA

In regard to basic principles for suggestion formulation, Harry Arons has developed an idea which may be called the "antonym technique." Arons appropriately notes:

> The suggestion should encompass the *desired result* -- it should *not* mention the *undesirable difficulty.* For example, let us say a student, when in the examining room, becomes *nervous, tense, upset* and the material he has learned becomes *blocked* in his mind. Underline the words which describe the difficulty he's having: *nervous, tense, upset, blocked.* List these words on a piece of paper and then, next to each word write down the *antonym* to it:

Word or Phrase	Antonym
NERVOUS	CALM
TENSE	RELAXED
UPSET	COMPOSED: TRANQUIL: SERENE
BLOCKED	FLOWS FREELY

> Now, form a sentence with the antonyms. Example: "When I am taking an examination, I am always calm, relaxed and composed, and whatever I have learned flows freely through my mind."

> What could be simpler? All problems can be handled in a similar way. [14]

It should be reiterated that *visual imagery* greatly stimulates and complements successful P.H.S.'s. It can also be used in combination with the above mentioned technique.

Classically, people who have had insight into the future and into themselves (for example, Adous Huxley) have been what may be called "right hemispherical people." They utilize their *computer child* with "maximum efficiency and minimal effort." They are often characterized as being intuitive, insightful, artistic, holistic, creative and imaginative. Huxley and his prolific writings, such as *The Doors of Perception* and *Brave New World,* are fine examples of these characteristics. In the selected papers of Milton Erickson, Erickson describes his encounter with Huxley, who was at the time deep in hypnosis. Huxley was a *focused dreamer* who had abundant insight into the very *real future* (See Appendix I).

It is the person who uses his imagination and who can envision (visualize) himself or his environment in the future who will be able to best adapt to the future's events. He can prepare for the future by choosing his goals and programming himself in a way that stimulates the realization and ultimate actualization of his potential.

In formulating your suggestions you should consider the laws, concepts and methodology of hypnosis, including the "antonym technique" and the use of visual imagery. While in hypnosis, one should "visualize" himself, doing, being, and "experiencing" what it is he wishes to realize he has achieved. This is the beginning of true belief established through hypnosis.

Remember, the subconscious receives input from all senses...see it, smell it, taste it, feel how it is to have achieved self mastery. You are realizing, internalizing and actualizing it more and more each day!

JUDGING THE DEPTH OF YOUR TRANCE

There are many ways to judge the depth of your trance. We can review the three basic trance depths: 1) the light or hypnoidal trance, 2) the medium or cataleptic trance and 3) the deep or somnambulistic trance. Let us briefly characterize these three trances further: "A" will symbolize the lighter degree of the particular trance depth and "B" will characterize the "deeper" (which leads to the next trance depth).

Light or Hypnoidal Trance (partial open-mind-edness):

A. Complete physical relaxation and eye cat-alepsy.

B. Catalepsy (rigidness) of the musculature (especially the limbs).

Medium or Cataleptic Trance (open-minded-ness):

A. Ability to follow most post-hypnotic sugges-tions.

B. Analgesia and partial amnesia (if desired)

Deep or Somnambulistic Trance (Hyper-open-mindedness):

A. Anaesthesia and Amnesia. Positive visual and auditory hallucinations. Usually, subject follows post-hypnotic suggestions completely.

B. Negative auditory and visual hallucinations.

Most self-hypnosis is done in the light and middle trance states. However, the goal of hetero-hypnosis is the deeper trance.

RULES OF P.H.S. FORMULATION

Cooke and Van Vogt (1965), in a well written and informative book, *The Hypnotism Handbook,* note what they consider to be the mechanics of self-hypnosis. They stress the following six points:

1) WRITE IT. Write the suggestion out in accordance with the laws of hetero-hypnotic therapy. Writing forces us to crystallize our ideas.

2) SYMBOLIZE IT. Give it a key word or idea, a code word. By definition then, the symbol represents the entire formulation.

3) EDIT IT. Read the written suggestion to insure that it complies with the basic laws. Revise it. Reconstruct it. Expand it. Condense it.

4) READ IT ALOUD. Reading aloud is preferable because it compels the uttering of each word.

In reading silently, we are accustomed to scanning and skipping.
5) HYPNOTIZE YOURSELF.
6) THINK THE SYMBOL. Make no effort to remember what the symbol means or to think of the original suggestion.

It must also be noted that, when using this methodology, one insures "waking" or *pre-hypnotic, hypnotic* and *post-hypnotic* results. Also, this method gives the subject an excellent alternative, which invariably works with the Law of Reversed Effect. When the "symbol" (or reminder/motivator image) is emotionalized, this method uses the Law of Dominant Effect, again complementing the positive effects of working with the Law of Reversed Effect.

PRE-SUGGESTION, MEMORIZATION AND THE EFFECTIVE USE OF A SYMBOL

As indicated by Cooke and Van Vogt (1965), the use of the *symbol* is very important. In the pre-suggestion period, before formally entering self-hypnosis, one can memorize and concentrate on the total "written" and "edited" P.H.S. The entire P.H.S. can be condensed into a single symbol. If a person's central presenting problem is depression, he may have quite a lengthy P.H.S. This entire P.H.S. could be symbolized and condensed into a single word, for example, "elation."

If he is to use this pre-hypnotic technique, the subject should remember that it is well to review (read and concentrate on) the written P.H.S. and consciously associate it with the particular symbol. With repetition, it will invariably be assimilated into the subconscious. In this pre-hypnotic period, the subject can use his conscious/analytical modality to wirte, symbolize, edit, read and memorize (internalize) his P.H.S.

What is important here is that, in hypnosis, the "analytical/defensive" part of the brain does not have to "bring you up" (making you lose trance depth) when you concentrate on a P.H.S. symbol. Whereas, with a "wordy"

P.H.S., the analytical/defensive modality is more activated. Hence, when using a *harmless* and *simple* symbol, cortical activity is reduced, since there simply is nothing to analyze or defend. The symbol is "intuited," the right hemisphere is more engaged, the computer child is passively instructed.

It would seem that conscious and analytical processes certainly deter and, to some degree, inhibit not only trance depth but also ultimate strength of the P.H.S. *By circumventing the analytical and the conscious mode with the simple symbol, opposing thoughts are, to a large degree, eliminated.*

In hetero-hypnosis, this technique is especially effective with people who reach only light and middle trances. These subjects need to keep their trance intuition and concentration at a relatively maximal level. They cannot afford to lose depth because of a lengthy and complicated P.H.S. The attendant response of the somnambulist, however, is much greater than that of the light or middle trance subject. The lengthy P.H.S. does not affect his trance in the same way that it does a "lighter" subject. In a sense, because he goes so "deep," he can afford to lose a little trance depth.

Again, we see the paradox of strength at work. The "weak" open-mindedness (suggestibility) of the somnambulist is his paradoxical strength. The "light trance" (often obsessive-compulsive and analytical) subject is so "strong" (defensive) that he is really weak! The "light" trance subject needs to let himself go! His resistance and defenses are obviated to a noticeable extent as the subject uses the less provoking symbol.

As has been inferred, even if the presenting problem or goal is complex, one should keep the symbol simple. A simple suggestion or symbol, no matter how paradoxically powerful, is "non-confrontive" to the analytical/defensive mode. The selective automatism and/or deautomatism of a certain response is thus enhanced by the use of the symbol, which subtly "reflects" the whole (Gestalt) P.H.S. Also conducive imagery and emotionalization of the symbol can foster the desired automatism/deautomatism.

By utilizing the symbol, the channel which leads to (what Coue called) the "outcropping of the unconscious" is more open and free-flowing. The pre-suggestions are more easily accepted and acted upon by the subconscious. Hypothetically speaking, the "right hemispherical mode" and "subconscious" accept more readily the symbol, since they are the storehouses of symbols, not of the analyzed word.

OPEN-MINDEDNESS TESTS AND UNIFORMITY

As we discussed earlier, open-mindedness increases one's capacity for hypnotic trance depth and success in accomplishing self-mastery. As Coue maintained, we must educate the imagination, not re-educate the will. We can achieve successful open-mindedness tests by keeping this in mind. There are many different kinds of open-mindedness tests that can be used in hetero and self-hypnosis.

The reader should keep in mind that if you do not "pass" an open-mindedness test, you will still do fine with hypnosis! In other words, don't get discouraged; you should move on to another test, still thinking positively and optimistically. At another time, you will be able to pass it. *Many people have "not" done well on these tests and still have had tremendous results with hypnosis.* One can look at them as another tool, helpful in achieving results with hypnosis, though not a necessity.

Essentially, what these tests do is to help the individual gain more and more control over his or her subconscious. In analogy, with repetition of successful tests, a person's subconscious and imagination become "slaves" to his conscious and will. To attain this, we must first "educate the imagination."

First, we will review two kinds of open-mindedness "test effects": 1) hypnotic and 2) post-hypnotic.

The hypnotic test effect: After you have put yourself into a relaxed state of being, or in light hypnosis, you can begin with your hypnotic open-mindedness test effect.

In stimulating the hypnotic (not post-hypnotic) open-mindedness test effect, it is good practice to suggest to yourself before doing the test that, "Immediately after I pass the hypnotic test (or when I say the hypnotic cue word), I will go three times deeper." An explanation of the "cue word" and of just when to use the test for a post-hypnotic effect is following.

Now, we will presume that you are in a "light" trance. You are deeply relaxed. The first open-mindedness test we will review is the hypnotic *eye catalepsy test.* It will be through this test that the author will demonstrate the two test effects (hypnotic and post-hypnotic). The methodology is analogous for all the open-mindedness tests and where one subject will prefer to use the eye catalepsy test, another may prefer to use quite another.

The eye catalepsy test can be used hypnotically or post-hypnotically. However, we will use it hypnotically first, since this is always the correct order for the beginner. (In self-hypnosis, a hypnotic open-mindedness test should preceed a post hypnotic test, until such time as the subject has conditioned himself to always manifest the desired and correct post-hypnotic response on the test.)

Now, tell yourself that 5-10 seconds after you have "passed" the eye catalepsy test, you will give yourself the hypnotic cue word which will "withdraw" the hypnotic test effect (in this case, eye catalepsy). This will become clearer as we continue.

Imagine and suggest to yourself that your eye lids have little lead weights on them...they are becoming tighter and tighter. They are glued shut...locked shut. And now, the more you try to open them, the tighter and tighter they get! Now, count to three, and *imagine* that each number locks them tighter and on three it will be absolutely impossible to open them...go ahead and try— they are glued shut!

Wait 5-10 seconds after you have counted to three and you have still not been able to open your eyes (the hypnotic test effect), and give yourself the hypnotic cue word. Maybe it is "apples." When you say "apples" (you should have previously suggested this to yourself), you will go three times deeper and your eyes are now normal and back in your conscious control. However, you will not open them, because you wish to go deeper still. After doing this test and passing it, (not being able to open your eyes and/or not seeing the light), you will find that each time you do it, it becomes easier and easier to pass.

The post-hypnotic test effect: After you have reassured yourself that your hypnotic test effect is successful, you can try it post-hypnotically (so that the effect occurs after self-hypnosis when you are *not* hypnotized). Thus, you can suggest to yourself (while in hypnosis) that for this test, "When I come out of hypnosis everything will be 'normal,' except that my eyes will be glued shut and I will not be able to open them" (until you say the cue word). As you can see, the difference is that now you are working on a post-hypnotic effect.

Give yourself another cue word and tell yourself (while still in hypnosis) that even though you will be out of hypnosis, it will be impossible to open your eyes until you say the cue word. You may say, "I will not be able to open my eyes when I am out of hypnosis until I say the word "trees." It is important to note that the author consistently uses a "1-3 count" for the hypnotic effect and a "1-5 count" for the post-hypnotic effect. This is because he prefers to use and uniformly does use a "1-5 count awakening" for all his hypnotic subjects.

The author would like to elaborate upon another important distinction. When doing this test for a post-hypnotic effect, the cue word should differ from the one used for the hypnotic effect. This is because the cue word of the hypnotic test suggests "going deeper," while the cue word of the post-hypnotic test implies that the subject is already "wide awake" and out of hypnosis. This is, of course, in addition to the removal of the eye catalepsy which both cue words accomplish. Though the cue words are different between the hypnotic and post-hypnotic test effects, it is critically important to always use the same respective cue word with the proper test effect. This is because, with practice, the cue words become symbolic suggestions for particular responses. There is a profound need here to be consistent and uniform. This is not only fundamental in the above context, but is true throughout the realms of hypnotism. For instance, the cue word "deep asleep," if used consistently and uniformly, will elicit the hypnotic trance without the lengthy verbal gymnastics of an hypnotic induction. With continual use, the subject voluntarily becomes automatized and falls swiftly into hypnosis by responding to the cue word, or what is also called the "instantaneous signal."

When doing another open-mindedness test, one should use the same cue word(s) at the appropriate time. That is, for the hypnotic test consistently use "apples" and for the post-hypnotic test effect use "trees." In this way, it becomes an integral part of your subjective repertoire, a kind of "visceral knowledge." We will go into another open-mindedness test after a brief note.

Hypnotic reaction or desire to pass the test? The author wishes to note at this time a certain phenomenon which occurs periodically. Sometimes a *new* patient has a question after self-hypnosis which goes something like this..."I felt very deeply relaxed and in some kind of a trance. I passed the open-mindedness test with both the hypnotic and post-hypnotic effect, but now I am not sure if the reason I passed it was because of a hypnotic reaction or because I want to pass the test to achieve deeper hypnosis and more self-mastery." When a question or statement of this type arises, it is invariably from a new patient whose hypnotic belief system and open-mindedness has not fully matured. The reconciliation of this simple ambiguity is merely practice.

This question is quite a normal reaction from the novice. Also, it is reasonable to assume that, at first, the positive manifestation of the hypnotic and post-hypnotic effect may be less, because of a desire to pass the test. However, in a short time, with practice and the paralleling effect of increased open-mindedness, trance deepening, and suggestion strengthening, this notion becomes absolutely irrelevant. With practice and uniformity, the manifestation of successful open-mindedness test reactions are clearly and purely a product of hypnotic trance conditioning.

As was just noted, the subject will find that passing these open-mindedness tests will become easier and easier. He also will go deeper, faster...just practice and allow it to happen...it will!

Once again, with regard to all open-mindedness tests, the subject should practice and strive for a noticeable and definitive post-hypnotic reaction. The post-hypnotic reaction will become strengthened (reinforced) with concommitant and consecutive successful test reactions.

The subject should begin to automatize himself, responding consistently and uniformly to cue words, such as the condensed P.H.S. symbol, "deep asleep" (for automatic induction), "wide awake" (for automatic awakening), "apples" (for "deepening" and removing an unwanted hypnotic effect), "trees" (as the subject is already "awake" and out of hypnosis, this cue word is essential for removing an unwanted post-hypnotic effect).

Lastly, it is "extremely easy" to pass the open-mindedness tests. Thus, it is hoped that the subject is not so obessively compulsive as to make it difficult. Remember that the underlying paradox of hypnotism is its "profound simplicity."

The heavy-lead arm test: Utilize the appropriate dynamics and concepts explained in the preceding section, beginning with "open-mindedness tests and uniformity." Relax yourself completely. Give your subconscious mind "permission" to positively react to your suggestions. For the *Hypnotic effect* suggest: "My right arm is light and normal. However, my left arm will become very heavy, like a lead pipe." Allow yourself to relax even more. Suggest to yourself, "my left arm is becoming more and more limp, slack and heavy. I am going deeper. My arm, shoulder and hand are becoming like lead...I can feel a kind of heavy rigidity." Continue (in your own words) to strengthen this notion.

Imagine and visualize a "horrendously large and bulky thick lead pipe, maybe a hundred times heavier than the weight of your entire body." Think of your arm as being like this pipe. Suggest to yourself that your arm feels, "heavier and heavier. I cannot even move my arm...it is as if it was stuck in the position that it is in...my left arm is deeply relaxed, so very heavy and tranquil. I am going to count to three and on three I will try to move it, but the more I try to move it, the heavier it becomes....

"After I pass this test, I will say the word 'apples' and my arm will return to normal, I will have full control over it and I will automatically go three times deeper.

"1. It is getting increasingly heavier... 2. Progressively becoming even more enormously heavy... 3. I can not move it... (5-10 seconds)..."apples!" ...I am drifting deeper and deeper...I have full control of my arm..."

With this procedure, the successful hypnotic test effect automatically deepens the trance. In so doing it allows for an even greater and more successful post-hypnotic effect, no matter what open-mindedness test is being used.

As with the eye-catalepsy test, the next step is to begin the *post-hypnotic effect.* Let us review this effect as applied to the *heavy-lead arm catalepsy test.* We will begin by suggesting that the cue word "trees" will release the arm from the post-hypnotic effect, in this case, extreme heaviness. The subject repetitively uses the same descriptive words (that is, for the left arm to become increasingly "heavy, limp," etc.), which have already been used in the hypnotic effect.

While counting to five, as the arm gets progressively heavier, the subject is at the same time "coming up" (out of hypnosis). On "five" two things spontaneously occur: A) He is aware, awake and totally out of hypnosis. (The eyes usually "spring open" when a subject "awakens" from hypnosis, provided he is not doing the eye-catalepsy test), and B) The subject finds that he absolutely cannot lift his arm up and if he does succeed in moving it, he does so only with a great deal of difficulty!

Success is ultimately defined by the degree of difficulty one has in "challenging" the P.H.S. test effect. Thus, if the subject *strains* to lift his arm (even though he may move it) this would indicate a fine and *successful* test result and that a positive effect had occurred.

If the arm does move slightly, the subject can reinforce the P.H.S. while being "awake" by repetitively autosuggesting (as he is physically and "consciously" trying to lift the arm): "more heaviness in my arm, heavier and heavier." If a new subject has a problem in passing a test, this "awake suggestion" procedure is advised.

For further open-mindedness ("suggestibility" and/or "hypnotizability") tests, the reader is advised to read Cooke and Van Vogt (1965), Fross (1974), Magonet (1976) and others (see Bibliography). Other tests may prove more effective and complementary.

These tests help the individual deepen his trance, strengthen his hypnotic technique and gain control over his imagination and subconscious. Successful results in

open-mindedness tests offer the subject a transitional
"touchstone" or a "channel," for converting the post-
hypnotic test effect into the therapeutic and situation-
specific post-hypnotic effect for self-improvement.

This can be done with a combination of common sense,
extrapolation from this text and others, and consistent
practice in self-hypnosis. *Remember, it is "not" necessary
to do open-mindedness tests. They should be viewed
as an additional tool that "can" be used.*

SECTION VIII

EXACT P.H.S. VERBALIZATIONS

A POINT OF PERSONALIZATION AND EXTRAPOLATION

The particular suggestions outlined here are for specific goals, habits or symptoms. They are relatively generalized, but sill to some degree effective.

What will stimulate maximum efficiency with minimal effort, with regard to attainment of a goal and/or the resolution of the habit or symptom, will be the "tailoring" and "personalizing" of the P.H.S. *That is, the suggestions in this section should be viewed as points of personalization and extrapolation.* They can be seen as examples to be modified with care and specificity for each individual.

When reviewing the section on "habits," a brief critique will often be made, underlining certain possible and common reasons why the problems exist. This is done in hopes that the reader will be able to incorporate this knowledge with both what has been written earlier and the insights he or she has gained from introspective analysis.

The reader is again advised not to discount the emotional need for a habit or symptom, which may be inappropriately used as a crutch or excuse. If you are having complications, you should certainly see a hypnotherapist. Remember, a habit or symptom cannot be removed (without symptom substitution) if the subconscious considers it necessary - this is a neurotic need, as compared with a superficial habit formation.

There will be good results if you allow yourself to truly believe in what you are doing. *Be aware and sense within. Tell yourself that you notice the improvement that grows and progresses every day, that you will be fully satisfied and happy with it and with yourself.*

Be consistent and memorize your P.H.S. Repeat your P.H.S. in and out of hypnosis and right before you go to bed. "Symbolize" it. Work on one thing at a time and do self-hypnosis at least twice a day until you have relieved your habit or symptom. Remembering the Law of

Reversed Effect, don't "push," you don't have to "make" it happen...let it happen...it surely will happen! You are there, you just have to realize it!

This section will be divided into two basic areas: 1) habits and 2) other maladies.

HABITS

Smoking:

The reasons for smoking seem to be multifaceted. Often one starts smoking to conform to his adolescent peer group. Though smoking physiologically makes the person more nervous, most smokers contend that it "relaxes them."

Case studies and interviews with patients demonstrate many common paralleling symptoms and aberrations: inability to relax, nervousness, often insecurity, need to have hands busy, often stress and frustration at work and/or home, lack of will power, sometimes sinus problems, shortness of breath, phlegm and coughing.

The smoker functions "automatically" with little awareness of what he or she is doing. The ego defense mechanisms of rationalization and denial are commonly used.

Therefore, one of the first suggestions is to become conscious of the habit of reaching for, lighting and puffing on a cigarette. You must interrupt that sequence, by catching the first action of reaching for the cigarette. You should consciously and deliberately ask yourself the question, "Do I really want it or is it just a habit?" Consider the question for a few seconds. Are you a robot or a human? If you do really want it, then do it—*But be aware of all of your actions.*

Light it...puff on it. Does it taste or feel good? Alright then, with the next puff ask yourself the same. Most normal people do not get any more pleasure beyond the second puff, especially when they are aware that this is so. Thus, put the cigarette out and forget it. Let yourself concentrate on something else. You have taken your first step toward self-mastery, human awareness and deautomatism. Major change *can* be problematic. A step by step approach is suggested. Psychological scientists have found that people attain *intrinsic* reward and pleasure by changing a little at a time (Haber, 1958).

Later on, if you wish to have a cigarette, become aware of why you want it. What stimulated the desire? Now, repeat the above process. Remember, you are a human, not a robot...you may now "choose" to have the next cigarette or not. You do not have to be a victim of habit, especially when there is not even any pleasure to be attained! Find a more meaningful pleasure substitute.

Visual imagery:

For example, first visualize yourself locked in a closet with tobacco smoke pouring in through a small hole. Imagine how hard it would be to breathe if only 5% of the closet space had oxygen in it. Concentrate on this: Imagine that it is totally dark and you think of getting out (stopping smoking). A "stop sign" flashes with a cigarette painted across it. (Continue this for five minutes). Then use positive visual imagery. Imagine walking through a beautiful tranquil wooded area. You enjoy the clean fresh air so much...feel yourself taking deep full breaths and your lungs expanding, etc. Then follow with your "personalized" P.H.S.'s, for example: "20 (first week), 15 (second week), 10 (third week), 5(fourth week) cigarettes are *more* than enough for me. They begin to taste foul and stale; I let them taste that way. I am, and will continue to be, completely relaxed and in complete control of my behavior. I will derive just as much satisfaction from my oral substitute and soon will not need it."

You can use any number of things for an oral (symptom) substitute - a clean pen, diet gum, toothpicks, straws, even a baby's nipple. Be inventive! Remember, in most cases, it's better to have an oral substitute than to "hit the ice box" and gain weight.

When it is finally your quit date (give yourself a realistic deadline) you may tell yourself:

P.H.S.:

"I feel totally aware and in control of my behavior. I am proud and happy to be a human and not a robot. I will remain a non-smoker and will allow myself to continue feeling naturally relaxed, fully satisfied and calm." (Like the A.A. view on alcohol, never have that first cigarette after you quit). "I have just had a fantastic enlightenment... I am free to breathe only fresh air!"

Symbol:

"free"

Weight:

The basic reasons people have weight problems are either organic, for instance, a thyroid dysfunction, or psychological/emotional, which is the usual case. One should consult with his physician to determine if there is an organic basis to the pathology; if there is not, then hypnosis is usually indicated.

As with smoking, case studies and interviews with patients demonstrate many common paralleling symptoms and aberrations. By far, smoking and weight control are the two most frequently presented problems at the author's office.

Eating because of one's anxiety, frustration and boredom is a common symptom and complaint. Especially noted among housewifes are "food binges," alcohol consumption, "junk food" snacking, especially in the late afternoons and after dinner.

In general, there is a lack of exercise, ("I have no will power" is often heard), lack of motivation, poor diet, high intake of starch, carbohydrates and sometimes sweets. Often there is shortness of breath, poor body and self image, sexual frustrations, feelings of guilt and inferiority. There is often emotional stress and depression (conflict) because of weight, eating when not hungry (negative automatism), and lack of energy. The ego-defense mechanisms of rationalization and denial are very common.

Again, like quitting smoking, losing weight is relatively easy if there are no deep-seated problems. Sometimes a behavioral (food intake) contract works well, using a balanced diet as its framework. Write a realistic contract stating what foods you will and will not eat and when. Then in hypnosis tell yourself: "I will be fully satisfied with my contract...I allow it to happen." (The author's record album or cassette tape has proven to be extremely helpful in this area.) *Allow yourself to feel full and think thin.*

Visual imagery:

Visual imagery in hypnosis could include seeing (visualizing) yourself after the weight loss: 1) with friends (male and female) admiring you for your "great looks," confidence, will power and composure or 2) Visualizing your mate or "desired lover'' being tremendously ''turned on'' sexually and emotionally toward you, or 3) Running naked on a long white sandy beach at the weight you are positively approaching. This is where you must personalize your P.H.S. based upon what will work best for you. Only you know this!

P.H.S.:

''Eating slower, I get much more satisfaction and contentment from less food. I am feeling healthier and have more energy and desire to walk, do exercise and play sports. I am aware that it takes less food to fill me. I have more will power and self-control and I am much more relaxed. I have a ''thin'' image of myself uppermost in my mind that I am actualizing. It is almost as if I drank a quart of water before and after each meal. Food is relatively unimportant.

Symbol:

''Thin''

Insomnia:

Insomnia is usually an easy problem to resolve. We live in an obsessive-compulsive environment and insomnia may be seen as a precipitant of this. It is a maladaptive habit.

The Law of Reversed Effect is important to mention here. You cannot ''make'' yourself sleep. You can, though, ''allow'' yourself to sleep.

Visual imagery:

Visual imagery may include visualizing yourself lying down on a high cloud which is drifting down an almost endless elevator shaft. See yourself peacefully floating past the 400th floor, then past the 399th floor, each time going deeper and deeper. Continue suggesting ''sleep'' after each number you visualize.

P.H.S.

"I am becoming so drowsy, tired and sleepy. From now on, I will fall asleep deeply and promptly. I am feeling so restful and totally relaxed. When I awaken, I will be wide awake and charged up." (use before the visual imagery).

Symbol:

"Sleep"

Nail-biting:

Nail-biting is usually associated with anxiety. Like other habits, at one point in time, there may have been a subconscious need for the symptom. However, in many cases, the subconscious need may be gone and only the symptom or habit remains.

The symptom is usually an "automatized" response, often beyond conscious awareness. At other times it may be a compulsive reaction of which the subject is aware, but finds hard to control.

Visual Imagery:

Visualize yourself: A mature adult in control of your behavior. Imagine your fingers are always coated with the worst taste you ever experienced. Visualize yourself sticking your fingers into a solution of this disgusting mixture three times a day.

Symbol:

"Mature"

Alcoholism:

This is very often a complicated problem, since the rationalization and denial system (ego-defenses) are usually strong. Family, social and environmental factors also contribute to the problem. Alcoholism often glazes over severe emotional or psychological problems. For best results, (if the person is able to confront and accept the fact that he or she is an alcoholic), the author suggests that the subject: 1) Join Alcoholics Anonymous (A.A.), and acknowledge openly the fact that he (or she) does have a drinking problem. 2) See a physician to be sure he is physically well. If your medical doctor agrees it is acceptable for you, the use of *antabuse* (a drug) will most assuredly stimulate revulsion to alcohol. 3) Seek out other professional help, possibly a psychiatrist, hypnotherapist or psychologist. Milieu and aversive therapy have proven to be effective. 4) In conjunction with the above, utilize the author's record album or cassette.

One approach using self-hypnosis is to focus on natural relaxation. Self-hypnosis can replace the "bottle." *Get high on hypnosis!* The person then should continue self-hypnosis 3-4 times daily (during initial "drying out period"). Even the moderate but consistent drinker will have a mild drying out period. Train yourself to do self-hypnosis before whatever circumstances would have previously evoked a drinking response (nervousness, tension, etc.). Use the author's recording during "happy hour" instead of drinking.

Once again, based upon the relatively poor remission rate of the "self-help" approach, the author suggests seeking professional help and using self-hypnosis as a supplement to it.

Visual Imagery:

A very plausible approach to the problem could utilize both positive and negative visual imagery. The positive side might include visualizing (in hypnosis) one's self in his favorite natural place (Grand Canyon, mountains, forest, stream, etc.) and becoming in harmony with it. Become aware that *you do not need alcohol when you are "relaxed."* Under hypnosis, negative V.I. can include re-experiencing the nausea and revulsion one has experienced when drinking too much alcohol. Visualize the drink and the bottle, then allow the noxious feeling to emerge as if you swallowed four repugnant, raw, rotten eggs and then a "drink of your usual." *Imagine* how disgusted you would feel!

P.H.S.

Personalize your P.H.S. For instance: "I will automatically associate the most disgusting smell, taste and sight I have experienced with alcohol. I am imagining them now...(pause)...it's horribly disgusting...vile and repulsive...I am fully in control of my behavior. I am relaxed and don't have to make excuses (rationalization and denial). I am contented and so happy to be myself and to be in natural harmony with nature. I am realizing my independence from alcohol. I am a human, not a robot. I control myself, and I am fully and completely satisfied!"

Symbol:

"Naturally high and free"

Drug Addiction:

The etiology of drug addiction is exceedingly similar to alcoholism. In many cases, the cause has a chronological referent. That is, one's "generation" or age group can, seemingly, determine whether, under the same dynamic conditions, one becomes an alcoholic or a drug addict. The influence of "peer pressure" is important. "Hard core" drug addiction is obviously more problematic than alcohol or excessive use of marijuana. Environmental and, to some extent, hereditary factors are also important. Hypnotic treatment procedures are most often identical to those for alcoholism.

The habits that have been elaborated upon here are probably the most common nationally. Once again, for best results, they are not to be reproduced and used as is. They represent a point of departure, personalization and extrapolation. The "exact verbalizations" part was written to stimulate the reader's ingenuity, inventiveness and to give him or her an idea of how to formulate P.H.S.'s.

An Important Note to All Readers:

In the preceeding "Habits" section, the reader was exposed to the often quite complicated causal background of different habits. The discussion of this, hopefully, stimulated some degree of sensitivity and understanding of what we are dealing with.

Since the focus of this book is on the proper development and formulation of P.H.S., not the underlying pathology and reasons for P.H.S., the following section will only furnish the reader with general P.H.S.'s for different presenting problems.

In the case of a specific aberration or pathology, and when looking at one's own presenting problem, the author strongly suggests an objective literary research into the problem. This, coupled with one's own introspective analysis, can serve as "solid ground" for one's own self-help therapy and self-improvement. Aldous Huxley once said, "Every man who knows how to read has it in his power to magnify himself, to multiply the ways in which he exists, to make his life full, significant and introspective." [15]

If it is economically feasible, the author also strongly recommends seeing a qualified hypnotherapist. This too, can be of tremendous benefit, both for insight into the problem and for methodological expertise and professional consultation.

To assist the reader with his literary research into his presenting problem, he will find listed after each of the following P.H.S.'s a reference book. These references form an excellent bibliography. It should be noted that the

P.H.S.'s herein are developed by the author and not in the reference books named.

OTHER MALADIES

Headaches:

P.H.S. (example) ''I am perfectly relaxed. Things flow freely. All the musculature of my scalp, face and head are going loose and limp. My fingers and toes are warming up, as if they were sweating under a warm blanket. I am so drowsy and sleepy.''

Reference:

Self-Hypnosis: Its Technique and its Use in Daily Living, pp. 171-179 (1976), by Leslie M. Lecron.

Anxiety:

P.H.S. (example) ''I am allowing myself to relax more and flow with things much more easily. My improvement becomes more noticeable with each passing day. I allow myself to enjoy myself and to be relaxed at home and at (school or work). I am in total control of myself.''

Reference:

Self-Hypnosis: A Conditioned Response Technique, pp. 173-218 (1976), by Laurance Sparks.

Marriage Problems:

P.H.S. (example, for husband *and* wife to use) ''I am an equal part of a whole. We are guided by our impressions of each other. My behavior evokes an impression in (name) and vice versa. If I expect him/her to change, I must change first. If I want to receive, I must first give. I am relaxed and contented.''

Reference:

Helping Yourself With Self-Hypnosis, pp. 164-172 (1976), by Caprio and Berger.

Sexual Dysfunctions:

P.H.S. (very general example) "I am relaxed and in control of my behavior. I feel good about myself and my partner and I believe sexuality is a natural, clean human process. Everything flows freely as if I was floating on a soft white cloud. I allow myself to enjoy more foreplay. I am fully satisfied with everything and less concerned about having an orgasm. It will arise spontaneously."

Reference.

Hypnosis and Behavior Modification: Imagery Conditioning, pp. 139-175 (1976), by Kroger and Fezler.

Self-control:

P.H.S. (example) "I have increasingly more self control and confidence in myself and in my abilities. Each day I realize that I am getting better and better. I control my subconscious and find more meaning in life."

Reference:

Psycho-Cybernetics, pp. 118-135 (1977), by Maxwell Maltz.

Phobias or Fears:

P.H.S. (general example) "I am profoundly relaxed. It is impossible for me to fear something when I am relaxed. I notice that when I visualize the feared object or situation, I am still relaxed... (pause and visualize feared object or situation)... each time I do self-hypnosis, it neutralizes me more and more. I feel free and tranquil. I am becoming increasingly more self-confident!"

Reference:
> *Hypnosis and Behavior Modification: Imagery Conditioning,* pp. 251-257 (1976), by Kroger and Fezler.

Nervousness:
> P.H.S. (example) "I am deeply relaxed and will continue to be so. I enjoy the tranquility of hypnosis. I am sleeping deeper at night."

Reference:
> *How To Use Auto-Suggestion Effectively,* pp. 114-119 (1976), by John Duckworth.

Stuttering:
> P.H.S. (example) "I am deeply relaxed and will continue to be so. I allow my speech to flow freely and naturally, as if I were alone. I have much more control and I speak carefully and slowly. My speech is getting better every day."

Reference:
> *Hypnotism Revealed,* pp. 82-85 (1976), by Melvin Powers.

Memory Learning and Recall:
> P.H.S. (example) "From now on, I am perfectly relaxed and clear headed. My mind is like a computer and I will allow it to work for me. I have confidence in my intelligence! Everything flows freely!"

Reference:
> *The New Self-Hypnosis,* pp. 196-206 (1976), by Paul Adams.

Depression:
> P.H.S. (general example) "I am deeply relaxed and I am aware that it's 'darkest before dawn' and that the warm sun is now progressively rising. Each day, I will find the good and positive in life. By concentrating on this, it will integrate into

me...a warm happy light. I am feeling much better and will continue to feel great!''

Reference:
Helping Yourself With Self-Hypnosis, pp. 134-143 (1976), by Caprio and Berger.

Emotional Scars:

P.H.S. (general example) ''I am completely relaxed. I am living in the here-now and am realizing more and more how lucky I am. I feel positively and happily independent. I can accept and 'work with' the past...it is desensitizing. I have converted poison into constructive medicine!'' I feel secure and self-confident.

Reference
Psycho-Cybernetics, pp. 136-153 (1977), by Maxwell Maltz.

Menstrual Pain:

P.H.S. (general example) ''I feel deeply relaxed and will continue to feel so. I am contented and feel good about all aspects of myself. Everything is flowing naturally and I am sleeping more soundly. I am aware of how relaxed I am in front of males and females. My muscles are becoming soft, slack and smooth.''

Reference:
A Handbook of Medical Hypnosis, pp. 292-301 (1968), by Ambrose and New Bold.

Becoming Successful:

P.H.S. (example) ''I am aware of the fact that I have an unlimited potential. I believe in my capabilities. From now on, I am going to do at least 20 percent better in everything I do. I have more and more self-confidence and self-assertion. I am successful!''

Reference:

> *The New Self-Hypnosis,* pp. 172-182 (1976), by Paul Adams.

Tics:

> P.H.S. (general example) "I am deeply relaxed. Every muscle, nerve and fiber is becoming more loose and slack. From now on, I will be more serene and placid in all situations. I will be pleased with my gradual progress. I will continue to be relaxed and in control."

Reference:

> *Post-Hypnotic Instructions,* pp. 38-39 (1969), by Arnold Furst.

Gastro-Intestinal Disorders:

> P.H.S. (general example) "My stomach muscles are profoundly relaxed. My organs are becoming 'smooth, warm and pink.' Everything is flowing freely. I am relaxing deeper and deeper. I am emotionally secure."

Reference:

> *Hypnosis and Behavior Modification: Imagery Conditioning,* pp. 394-403 (1976), by Kroger and Fezler.

Pain:

> P.H.S. (very general example) "I know that if I am totally relaxed I can experience great pleasure and serenity. I am relaxing more and more each day and I am realizing how good I feel. It is as if I had novocain and lubricant injected into that certain part of me."

Reference:

> *Self-Hypnotism: The Technique and Its Use In Daily Living,* pp. 131-140 (1976), by Leslie M. LeCron.

Asthma:

P.H.S. (general example) "I am becoming more independent and I accept the responsibilities of being an individual. I am safe, secure, very relaxed and I am realizing that my breathing is going smoothly and easily. I have more and more self-confidence! Things that have happened in the past are resolved. I am a new person."

Reference:

Hypnotism, p. 169 (1957), by G.H. Estabrooks.

High Blood Pressure:

P.H.S. (example) "My blood pressure is gradually lowering to normal. I am becoming much more relaxed. I feel safe and contented. My ability to relax myself and control my blood pressure gets better with each hypnosis session."

Reference:

Post-Hypnotic Instructions, pp. 126-129 (1969), by Arnold Furst.

Arthritis and Calcium Deposits:

P.H.S. (example) "I am becoming more relaxed. I feel a pleasurable sensation going through my body...a green organic light. From now on, each time I move my previously affected area, a drop of lubricant will saturate it. Everything goes smoothly and effortlessly."

Reference

Post-Hypnotic Instructions, pp. 129-131 (1969), by Arnold Furst.

Hypertension:

P.H.S. (example) "I am becoming more relaxed and emotionally stable. I am allowing the entire musculature of my body to relax deeper than ever. Each day, I will be aware of the fact that I am more relaxed. I will let myself become more tranquil. I am cured and healthy!"

Reference:
> *Hypnosis and Behavior Modification: Imagery Conditioning,* pp. 351-355 (1976), by Kroger and Fezler.

Acne and Emotionally Caused Skin Problems:
> P.H.S. (general example) ''I feel deeply relaxed and will continue to feel so. I am contented with myself and feel good about all aspects of myself. Everything is flowing naturally and I am sleeping more soundly. I am aware of how relaxed I am in front of males and females. My skin is becoming soft and smooth.''

Reference:
> *A Handbook Of Medical Hypnosis,* pp. 292-301 (1968), by Ambrose and New Bold.

Frustration:
> P.H.S. (example) ''I am becoming deeply relaxed. I am now able to ''go with'' things. I am more and more aware of the fact that I have a tremendous capacity to transcend myself into profound tranquility and at the same time cope with the profanities of life.''

Reference:
> *The Relaxation Controversy,* pp. 90-100 (1976), by Martin Ebon.

Death:
> P.H.S. (general example): ''I am a reflection of the universe, a facet of time and space. In Taoism, there is only heaven and earth; I will enter heaven as did my good friend(s). I am letting it out now and cry for my friend... (pause). I feel only serenity and convergence with The Greater. I am meditating on this.''

Reference:
> The *Tao Te Ching.*

A CONCLUDING FOOTNOTE: SYMPTOMS NOT COVERED

Once again, the author cannot overemphasize the ultimate and unprecedented effectiveness of the combination of this book and the recording (album or cassette tape). For best results, it is strongly advised that the reader purchase a copy of the recording and use it in combination with the knowledge obtained from this book, integrating theory with personal application. The author also suggests a consistent use of progressive relaxation, no matter what the goal or problem is. This will increase trance depth and the effectiveness of one's P.H.S.

The writer has recorded a special cassette tape on "progressive relaxation" (request more information by writing to the address on the last page). There are also several good books available which are helpful in this area.

Unfortunately, space limits the number of examples and background information in this book. More common problems, such as smoking, weight and alcohol abuse demanded a more indepth review. Again, because of space limitations, less common and more complicated problems simply could not be investigated. Also, there are many P.H.S.'s for every problem to be solved. This is why self-knowledge and "personalized" P.H.S.'s are so important.

For habits, symptoms or maladies not elaborated upon previously, or for further information concerning a problem, the reader may write the author (at the address on the last page) requesting professional assistance. The reader can explain and send a brief description of the problem to be overcome and his goals, along with ten dollars. In this case, the author will reply by sending a background survey of the problem with possible solutions, along with several other P.H.S.'s. Another alternative is to mail twenty-five dollars with the written problem and request that the author send the above material, together with a "personalized" hypnotic cassette tape which includes the induction, deepening, "specific" P.H.S.'s and awakening. This is done as a professional courtesy for the reader.

NOTES

[1] Bhak Tive Danta Swami Prabhupada, *Bhagavada-Gita* (New York: Collier Books, 1972) p. 313.

[2] Fromm, E., *The Art of Loving* (New York: Harper & Row Publishing Co., 1962) pp. 73-74.

[3] *Ibid.*

[4] Watts, A., *Psychotherapy East and West* (New York: Ballantine Books, 1974) p. 40.

[5] Kroger and Fezler, *Hypnosis and Behavior Modification: Imagery Conditioning* (Philadelphia: J.B. Lippincott Co., 1976) p. 4.

[6] Duckworth, J., *How to Use Auto-Suggestion Effectively* (N. Hollywood: Wilshire Book Co., 1976) p. 157.

[7] Norwood, W. D., *The Judoka* (New York: A. Knopf Inc., 1973) p. 44.

[8] Duckworth, J., *How To Use Auto-Suggestion Effectively* (N. Hollywood: Wilshire Book Co., 1976) p. 104.

[9] *Ibid,* p. 106.

[10] Kubose and Ogura, *Zen Koans* (Chicago: H. Regnery Co., 1973) p. 98.

[11] Duckworth, J., *How To Use Auto-Suggestion Effectively* (N. Hollywood: Wilshire Book Co., 1976) pp. 151-152.

[12] Adams, P. T., *The New Self-Hypnosis* (N. Hollywood: Wilshire Book Co., 1976) p. 101.

[13] *Ibid,* pp. 93-96.

[14] Arons, H., *How To Formulate Suggestions For Hypnosis and Self-Hypnosis* (New Jersey: Power Publishers, 1976) pp. 17-18.

[15] Caprio and Berger, *Helping Yourself With Self-Hypnosis* (New York: Prentice-Hall, 1976)

APPENDIX I

THE SELF-FULFILLING PROPHECY AND MAGICAL THINKING

Though Freud considered himself a "cheerful pessimist," few professionals including mainstream psychoanalysts find much of the psychoanalytical perspective at all cheerful. Psychoanalysis, in fact, is a rather pessimistic conception as a whole.

Freud wrote an essay, *The Future of an Illusion,* in 1927. At the time of this writing, Freud was approximately seventy and agonized with cancer of the jaw. This cancer ultimately proved to be the cause of his death in years to come. Along with this personal trauma at the time of his writing, he also suffered from the deaths of several close friends and loved ones. In this essay Freud inappropriately stepped out of his own area of specialization and condemned organized religions. He considered them to be man's strongest crutch. He thought religion to be centered around wish-fulfillment. Freud considered wish-fulfillment to be a tension-reducing object. Dreams in themselves were wish-fulfillments. We dream about what we want.

It is easy enough to believe that we dream about or imagine what we want, however the Freudian conception negates its own result. The irony can be seen when one considers the fact that Freud utilized his imagination as a vehicle to write, formulate and even speculate about his theories. That is, given the empirical, objectively verifiable, experimental evidence one must, as Freud did, "envision" the framework of this material.

When we are born we come into the world with a blank slate (tabula rasa). As children, we accept almost all suggestions and impressions from our parents and other authority figures as being real both consciously and subconsciously. As the child matures, these suggestions are strengthened. Gradually, in a like manner, the child accepts suggestions and impressions from peer groups, teachers, mass media, etc. The problem is that many of these influences have a negative and deleterious effect upon maturation and psychological health in the here/now and in the future of the individual. One self-fulfills both the negative and positive suggestions and impressions.

In the notion of magical thinking, thinking something is the same as doing it. Thinking and imagining it leads to the fulfillment of certain wishes. Freud mistakenly had a pessimistic outlook upon wish-fulfillment and magical thinking, although it was by using a discriminated (not generalized) type of magical thinking that he conceived his theories and won acclaim. For instance, *The Interpretation of Dreams,* by Freud, demonstrates his own kind of magical thinking—imaginative, artistic and creative. However much aware of it, he envisioned himself as a great thinker and self-fulfilled his own prophesy via focused and creative magical thinking.

This author believes that as the self-fulfilling prophesy can have a positive or negative effect upon the individual, so too can magical thinking. In many cases, the self-fulfilling prophesy and magical thinking are analogous. This author attributes most of his positive accomplishments to what he calls "creative, focused and discriminated magical thinking." This is a delineation which Freud did not take into account. Freud's concept was based upon a magical thinking which was generalized, indiscriminated and contained omnipotence of thought.

One can wish and can magically think in a way which "realistically" helps oneself therapeutically. This is not schizophrenia nor a thought disturbance! It is a means to a proper end product. What is schizoid, however, is the consequence of negative suggestions which we have unconsciously accepted. "Creative, focused and discriminated magical thinking" is a way to reprogram the computer child (ourselves) and resolve the results of negative suggestions and impressions.

In self-hypnosis, while resolving the effects of pathogenic suggestions and impressions, the new positive magical script becomes more real with each passing day. Before long, it is no longer magical but positively self-fulfilled. It is complementary and therapeutically real!

Oversimplified as it may seem, one could say that the reason Jung left Freud was because of Freud's over-emphasis on sexuality and his pessimistic and negative view of magical thinking. In a sense, where Freud belittled it, Jung elevated it. For more related information, read: *How Your Past Life Can Help You Now* by Van Warrebey and Koblenzer.

Throughout the world, religions use a form of magical thinking which sparks positive self-fulfillment. In most cases, this magical thinking is not a crutch but rather a means to enlightenment. These religions use words such as envision, imagine, visualize, foresee, etc. These conceptual tools are exceptionally effective in the science of hypnotism and self-hypnosis.

We are motivated by what we desire and envision. The student gains motivation by imagining himself graduating and all the benefits of being a graduate. For this to occur, his desire and motivation must outweigh other blocks and resistances. Likewise, to kick a habit one finds that his desire and motivation must be stronger than the resistance of the habit. By imagining or envisioning something that motivates us, we can use this "inner strength" to combat resistance and gain self-mastery. In self hypnosis this motivation becomes magnified because we are relaxed and are concentrating on it. The imagination is focused upon a certain positive idea, and when one does this consistently in self-hypnosis it becomes ingrained in the subconscious and becomes self-fulfilled.

The Bible says, "What you believe in your heart, so shall it be done unto you." If we exchange the word "subconscious" for the word "heart," we have a twentieth century conceptualization which is commensurate with the underlying theory and structure of hypnotism.

Not long ago, this author was teaching a course for

doctors who wished to use hypnosis in their practice and become hypnotherapists. One young doctor, who knew quite well the laws and principles of hypnosis, had a great deal of difficulty with assertion when hypnotizing a subject. He lacked self-confidence. His choppy voice was quivering, his hands were shaking and his command of language and voice inflection was terrible. He unknowningly transmitted his lack of self-confidence to the subject. As a result of this, the subject was so uncomfortable that she could not become adequately hypnotized. Minutes later, this author hypnotized the doctor and gave him a P.H.S. that he had a fantastic amount of self-confidence as if he had been hypnotizing subjects for ten years. The doctor then came out of hypnosis and proceeded to hypnotize quite readily the same subject with whom he had had such difficulty. The results were amazing! The young doctor did excellently and continued to get progressively better. The P.H.S. had stimulated a positive true belief, which replaced a negative and pathogenic one. He believed subconsciously that he was self-confident!

With the acceptance of the seemingly magical P.H.S., the doctor was able to triumph over his subconscious feelings of inferiority which were a result of earlier learning. Once again, the problem was the subconscious acceptance of negative suggestions and impressions which in time stimulated a pathological self-fulfilling prophesy. The doctor was given an alternative magical script which he positively self-fulfilled and made real.

APPENDIX II

JESUS, HYPNOSIS AND AWARENESS BRIDGES

In considering the content and philosophy of this book and this appendix, several factors weighed heavily on my mind. For instance, I am aware that by taking a theological or meta-scientifical position, I am at the same time "turning off" several readers and prospective readers. That is, by saying nothing with regard to Jesus, I would materialistically gain more.

Likewise, several years ago, while taking a college course in speech making, I learned that the paradoxical and main technique (or trick) politicians use, is to say nothing and really make it sound fantastic. By saying something and taking a clear stand, they offend some whom they would not offend by saying nothing. Not only this but, by saying "something," it puts them in a position where if they do not do this something, providing they are elected, they could possibly not be reelected. Whether it is a trick or technique really only depends on one's status and the letters after one's name!

Despite the criticism from my professional peers, readers, etc., of my not being scientific, I am going to reflect a theological stand. The consequences of this action are outweighed by the ultimate and innate good in the position. People have received therapeutic results from religion and Bible study for thousands of years before the concepts of Psychology and Psychotherapy were coined in the last century.

As an alternative to this topic, I had also considered writing an appendix on what I call *awareness bridges and robot walls.* Though this concept is less important, it is still worthy of a brief review.

Essentially, a primary flaw in operant conditioning is that punishment stimulates aggression and moreover, punishment is ineffective as a deterrent to psychopathic or sociopathic behavior (e.g., prison recidification). Extrinsically "corrected" behavior (via punishment) extinguishes, if further negative reinforcement (punishment) is not given continually. Once again, negative reinforcement loses its effect and stimulates aggression.

The other strata which is questionable is the notion of extrinsic reward used in operant conditioning and behavior modification. To their dismay, Behaviorists have found that once extrinsic reward is removed the motivation of the organism to perform diminishes (McMahon, 1977). However, the *results of intrinsic reward are much better, both in terms of duration and intensity.* We must also keep in mind that the operant conditioning paradigm is ineffective in accounting for the natural tendency in humans and lower organisms to be *curious* and that we often *do things for the sake of doing them.* (Harlow *et. al.,* 1956)

The concept of existential automatism and deautomatism suggests utilizing an intrinsic reward system (e.g., self-mastery). Next, it suggests using an extrinsic reward system only to change a here/now behavior. However, one should take steps to positively change behavior right away (extrinsically) and while in this process, one should introspect and contemplate upon what intrinsic motivators would be more long-lasting for him or her.

This is where *awareness bridges* and their explicit deautomatism are necessary to replace *robot walls* (defenses, habits or blocks). People need to realistically become aware of themselves and their behavior. This may seem self-evident, however, most people are existing so much unaware of why they are doing what they are doing. Some prefer to "cop-out" with a "blissful state of ignorance" which is in itself a mammoth robot wall.

For one to become aware enough to hurdle and bridge beyond his robot wall(s), one needs to have time to reflect, meditate or pray (deautomatize). Higher consciousness is itself intrinsically rewarding. This clears the mind and often is a passive stimulant fostering "aha effects," insight, awareness and uniquely productive thought. For instance, the concepts of the *computer child* and *existential (or selective) automatism/deautomatism* was a result of such meditation...a dream fulfilled and polished.

Paradoxically, even by doing nothing one can also do something productive! The Taoists write: "The way (Tao) in its course does nothing and in so doing there is nothing it does not do." A profound by-product of meditation (a type of deautomatism) and such is *learning consolidation.* That is, learning theorists (McGaugh, 1967) have found that periods of doing nothing (e.g., resting or sleeping) allows learned material to solidify in the memory storage system. This of course works with the Law of Reversed Effect. Time to reflect, meditate and rest will someday be incorporated into the context of the school day.

Positively conceptualized awareness bridges transcend the resistance and conflict of self and goal. Like in Herrigel's book, *Zen In the Art of Archery,* the target becomes an extension of one's self. In another way, you are there and every day you become more aware of it! You are unfolding like a flower toward its ultimate fruition. Awareness and reassessment are extremely important.

I believe that people have a need, an innate and intrinsic desire, which is converted into motivation, for self-improvement. In many cases, extrinsic reward and punishment is not only ineffective for positive and long-lasting behavioral and psychological change, it is unnecessary. It is obviously unnecessary when one achieves durable self-mastery through his own intrinsic motivators. Self-improvement is its own intrinsic reward. One can view interest and motivation as being intrinsic (Levin and Fasnacht, 1974). If people did not innately strive toward self-improvement, this book and other "How To" books would not be in existence. Also, in many cases, *curiosity* begets self-knowledge and self-knowledge begets self-improvement.

The Oriental psycho-philosophy and related close family Way of life is to a large degree a function of intrinsic reward. Honor, meaning, skill, pride, purpose in life and higher consciousness are themselves "beyond freedom and dignity" in a very positive sense. We in the West critically need a new and more *meaningful* model for *pleasure!*

As opposed to negative needs (sex, hunger, thirst, etc.), which may imply our seeking to satisfy a lack within ourselves, positive needs are caused by neither deprivation nor external reward; in this case there is a non-tissue need for and intrinsic reward from the self-improvement act itself. Maslow says that humans have higher goals and motivations than animals. He claims that self-esteem leads to the final need of self-actualization (which are themselves intrinsically motivating and rewarding).

The causeway of life can be vividly symbolized for twentieth century technological man by the train and station. For several years, as a student at Rutgers University, I was a participant in the rush-hour commuting syndrome. I would, several times a week, journey by railroad from the country to the city and back again. What I observed was not at all inspiring for a young, idealistic and energetic student.

The frustrated commuter seemed, to me, to be totally unaware of what he was doing. On the "train of life," he seemed to be neatly tucked away in his newspaper, rather than being at all aware of the panoramic scenery on his way. He seemed to be constantly and obsessively analyzing "important things," but to no apparent avail. He was always running, although I was not sure if it was *to* or *from*. Maybe it was both!

A casual observer might speculate that these people had no desire for self-improvement. However, upon interviewing many of the commuters, I was surprised to find that each in their own way was doing something which they considered to be self-improving. They were, however, in so many cases operating within the robot wall mode.

Some of these people kept in touch with me. We discussed the concepts of awareness bridges and robot walls during our relationship. Each one agreed that by deautomatizing and more realistically being aware of themselves they were able to *see* other alternatives and to increasingly exercise their freedom of choice. Awareness bridges symphonically got them from one place to another and they disclosed that they began to enjoy getting there! In effect, they opened their eyes to appreciate the exquisitely simplistic view on their Way. Some claimed that they got more meaning out of life and that this itself was a source of motivation and inspiration. Others maintained that awareness bridges led to their communication with that something greater....Jesus!

I believe in a kind of Theological Psychology and especially in a Theological Psychotherapy. In the future, I would say that almost all General Psychology textbooks for college students will contain a chapter on this viable subject and theoretical perspective. Being a college professor, and having reviewed many General Psychology textbooks, I have found an amazing deficiency in this area. The pendulum will swing back toward the consideration and support of this perspective. An instructor or professor who includes this point of view in his lecturing/teaching is aware of this fact.

As I inferred earlier, true belief and common sense are rare qualities of our culture, especially in the realms of academia. This is partially because Psychological Theory and Social Law are in a state of flux and probably will be for some time. The only immutable law is Nature and God!

We live in a world of rapidly changing scientific and social "truths." Western man has developed an apparent failure to "believe" in almost anything wholeheartedly, including himself! He does have one quasi-belief though. He believes in a pseudo-god on earth...materialistic (extrinsic) rewards.

Therapeutic religious institutions that for centuries supplied intrinsic reward and satisfied Western man's "belief needs" have been seriously protested and questioned. In most cases, these "belief needs" have been circumvented by a more pleasure seeking and hedonistic life style. Unfortunately, this life style is in itself dualistic, static and meaningless. It is simply harder to receive intrinsic reward under these conditions. Its constituent must face an extrinsically rewarding and punishing reality which is self-limiting and conflicting with progressive change. Though egocentric pleasure attainment and hedonism are gratifying at their apex moments, this lifestyle severely lacks meaning and elicits existential anxiety.

Ironically, "strong" Western man who paradoxically lives in a most complex and rapidly changing society is highly resistant to change. He wishes to resolve this dilemma but he is in a rut—a vicious circle. He is so strong and resistant that he is totally inflexible and often in conflict with his rapidly moving society.

Though man is naturally psychologically and physically *endoskeletal* (soft outside, hard inside), Western man has developed an *exoskeletal* (hard outside, soft inside) type of personality structure. Thus, extrapolating from Eastern philosophy such as Taoism, an exoskeletal personality is paradoxically weak.

There is an ironic and pathogenic need for behavioral predictability in the West, where the defensive exoskeletal personality is positively reinforced, and appropriate. People like B.F. Skinner would like everyone to be an obedient robot. People intuitively know there is more to life than being robotic! Jesus is a way to inner rest and theological psychotherapy. Jesus is an integrating and immutable presence.

The Bible can bring meaning to everyone's life. It is intrinsically rewarding! Jesus is in you if you allow him to be. A personal God or integrating presence is a notion which synthesizes a more pure and complementary relationship between the individual and the universe.

The exoskeletal personality and chaotic perception of the world tends to desolve incrementally with a Jesus-centered-meta-self-hypnosis. Jesus is the most wholesome and effective Hypno-therapist! Jesus can help you on your way. He can be your personal awareness bridge.

With the belief need fulfilled, the subject is able to "flow with" life more adaptively, as he existentially becomes more endoskeletal. That is, he becomes more naturally himself and spiritually in tune.

In Hypnotherapy, the subject is introduced to a new outlook on life—an intuitive meta-hypnotic perspective. As sessions continue, the hypnotherapist will observe a profound decrease in his patient's defenses and resistances. The patient has an "aha effect"—an enlightenment.

He has never lost *It* and he becomes more aware of *It* every day!

The patient's Way (Tao) of life receptively flows with It. He flows with Jesus. This stimulates a wholesome manifestation of the individual's harmony with life and Jesus, the Integrating and Immutable Presence. Jesus is the God-Law. The endoskeletal personality finds real strength and few conflicts; for who or what can conflict with that which is truly supple and receptive?

When the patient has become truly receptive to the notion of his transmutation with God or, if you will, with The Integrating and Immutable Presence, he at the same time truly believes. In therapy, at this point, true belief sparks its own therapeutic fulfillment and the sessions may become less frequent. The patient becomes more integrated, self-sufficient, and also spiritually and psychologically more healthy.

I further believe in and personally approach life with a kind of *judo* (Gentle Way) *epicureanism*. That is, I believe that people can put themselves in a position of relative flexibility and choice, which allows them to more gracefully *flow* through life with least resistance. The strict epicurean may define resistance as being unpleasant or discomforting. I believe this needs a more positive redefinition, as this will stimulate its own self-fulfillment! The directionality of this flow is toward a *purposeful pleasure* and meaningful reward through self-mastery.

APPENDIX III

CREATIVITY AND SELF-MOTIVATION

The creativity of the right hemisphere is extremely important, especially with regard to the fact that 1) creative people are more intrinsically motivated and 2) extrinsic rewards have less meaning for creative people (Nicholls, 1972). *We in the West need to learn to positively "break set" (deautomatize) and become more creative in our approach to and interpretation of life (reality).* Creative people are more self-motivated. In the future, industrial as well as clinical psychologists will utilize the creativity of the individual to help him achieve more harmony, meaning and motivation. Once again, people in the West need to *balance* their right and left hemispheres (e.g., I.Q. with creativity).

Ironically, our society "professes" staunch *individualism,* yet it seemingly rewards only robot conformity and obsessive analytical (non-creative/intuitive) thinking. In the East, possibly because of the closeness of *family, state and tradition,* the creative/artistic archetype and his innate sensitivity is intrinsically and extrinsically rewarded (e.g. for his uniqueness and creative endeavor). This same archetype in the West is often rebellious, suppressed, manipulated, and a victim of intellectual/analytical prejudice. This I.Q. (left hemispherical) prejudice is ironically seen within the very institutions which profess to teach "clinical" psychology. (For instance, G.R.E. and

M.A.T. tests as the determinants of acceptance into graduate schools.) Much less "testable," intuitive intelligence, creativity and sensitivity are most often circumvented for high I.Q. and book knowledge. In our quantitative and test oriented society, the creative/artistic archetype is in a sense being chastized for the system's inability to develop a valid and reliable standardized creativity test.

The schizoid society labels the creative person bizarre, unusual and indifferent. The underlying paradox and irony is that to be truly sane, one must become "abnormal," as interpreted by mass society! The creative/artistic archetype rejects the strongly negative (hypnotic-like) suggestion that he is nothing and must conform to the lunacy of robotism, obsessive compulsiveness, excessive apathy and left-hemispherical fixation.

APPENDIX IV

LETTING GO, JUDO AND BEGINNING A NEW WAY OF VIEWING SELF

The climax of Judo is in the *letting go.* "Letting go" is itself a transcendance of mechanism and manipulation. It is uniquely and intrinsically rewarding, if one allows oneself to realize it! One's apparent opposition in Judo is like the resistance of a habit and or negative thought. It can be viewed and treated similarly. Metaphorically speaking, in throwing his opponent (resistance), the judoka (judo student) learns that he cannot analytically "make go", he must spontaneously "let go". To master the "Gentle Way", he must *change his viewpoint* from opposition and competition, and "give way" to coopera- tion and harmony. He finds his inner strength in simplicity and suppleness. This perception of the world stimulates a therapeutic *self-discipline* which is extremely meaningful, self-perpetuating and intrinsically rewarding. It is a wholesome and healthy Way of the Life physically, psychologically and spiritually.

An old Japanese story comes to mind of a donkey who was tied by rope to a post. The more the jackass *tried* to *make* himself get away from the post, the more he choked himself and found he was stuck. The post of course could be a symbol for anything (e.g. cigarettes, garbage food, drugs, a neurotic need, self-limitations, etc.). With his disillusionment, the donkey *quit trying,* sat down (deautomatized) and *forgot about* the rope and post. This action produced a new viewpoint and a different perspective. At that same moment, the rope began to loosen and he was quite surprised to find that he could slacken it *without trying.* In time, the rope became so loose that with a slight twist of his neck and head he cast off his burden and then walked away happy and contented. The donkey had thrown the rope! In analogy, he let go by deautomatizing, going with and "re-viewing" the essential nature of the *interaction* between his true-self and that which "seemingly" was a source of resistance.

The liberation was attributable to the purpose becoming purposeless, the goal goalless and the effort effortless. One can find the strength of letting go, by *allowing* himself to change his view of himself...it is a metamorphosis of conception and strength. The end result is pliant yet durable inner-strength, which works *with* and *for* the individual, not against him. This is the judo of self-control and self-mastery.

NOTES

NOTES